JOAN OF ARC
and the Hundred Years' War in World History

William W. Lace

Enslow Publishers, Inc.

40 Industrial Road   PO Box 38
Box 398   Aldershot
Berkeley Heights, NJ 07922   Hants GU12 6BP
USA   UK

http://www.enslow.com

Library of Congress Cataloging-in-Publication Data

Lace, William W.

    Joan of Arc and the Hundred Years' War in World History / William W. Lace.

        p. cm. — (In world history)

    Summary: A biography of the fifteenth-century peasant girl who led a French army to victory against the English, witnessed the crowning of King Charles VII, and was later burned at the stake for witchcraft.

Includes bibliographical references and index.

    ISBN 0-7660-1938-1

    1. Joan, of Arc, Saint, 1412–1431—Juvenile literature. 2. Christian women saints—France—Biography—Juvenile literature. 3. Hundred Years' War, 1339–1453—Juvenile literature. 4. France—History—Charles VII, 1422–1461—Juvenile literature. [1. Joan, of Arc, Saint, 1412–1431. 2. Saints. 3. Women—Biography. 4. Hundred Years' War, 1339–1453. 5. France—History—Charles VII, 1422–1461.] I. Title. II. Series.

DC103.5 .L33 2003

944'.026—dc21

                                 2002006331

Printed in the United States of America

10 9 8 7 6 5 4 3 2 1

To Our Readers:

We have done our best to make sure all Internet Addresses in this book were active and appropriate when we went to press. However, the author and the publisher have no control over and assume no liability for the material available on those Internet sites or on other Web sites they may link to. Any comments or suggestions can be sent by e-mail to comments@enslow.com or to the address on the back cover.

Illustration Credits: Enslow Publishers, Inc., pp. 4, 7, 16, 47, 59, 60, 72, 110; Hulton Archive/Getty Images, pp. 10, 22, 27, 32, 40, 41, 45, 48, 55, 83, 101; Reproduced from the Collections of the Library of Congress, pp. 35, 91.

Cover Illustration: © Digital Vision, Inc. All rights reserved (Background Map); Reproduced from the Collections of the Library of Congress (Joan of Arc Portrait).

Contents

1 The Marketplace 5

2 The Endless War 12

3 Domrémy 26

4 Chinon 38

5 Orléans 50

6 Reims 63

7 Paris and Compiègne 74

8 Rouen 85

9 The Triumph of France 99

10 Redemption and Legacy 108

Timeline 114

Chapter Notes 118

Further Reading and
    Internet Addresses 126

Index 127

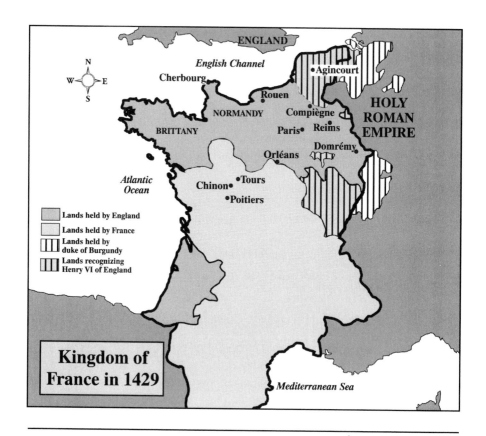

Kingdom of France in 1429

England and France fought the Hundred Years' War over control of certain areas in France. Most of the cities and villages important to the war and the quest of Joan of Arc were located in northern France, which was controlled by England.

Chapter 1

The Marketplace

The English soldiers were bored—bored and hungry. Since early morning, they had been standing on the cobblestones of the old marketplace of the French city of Rouen. Would this execution ever take place?

There was nothing very unusual about the English being in a French city. Since 1337, the two countries had been fighting what would someday be known as the Hundred Years' War. Now it was Wednesday, May 30, 1430, and no one in Rouen could remember a time when English soldiers were not marching through the French countryside or attacking French towns.

There were three platforms in the marketplace. The judges sat on one, the priests on another. From the third and tallest rose a stake surrounded by bundles of wood. At the top of the stake was a sign reading, "Joan the Maid, liar, pernicious, seducer of the people, diviner, superstitious, blasphemer of God, presumptuous, misbelieving in the faith of Jesus Christ, idolator, cruel, dissolute invoker of devils, apostate, schismatic and heretic."[1] A lengthy list, indeed, for a nineteen-year-old girl.

Symbols of Disgrace

Jeanne d'Arc, Joan of Arc in English, had been led, weeping, from her cell and put in the executioner's cart for the short journey to the marketplace. She wore a long, black dress. Her head, shaved as a sign of remorse for wrongdoing, was topped with a paper hat—a mockery of the pointed hats worn by bishops. The hat bore a sign proclaiming her a relapsed heretic, that is, a person who, having renounced crimes against the Catholic Church, has resumed them. Both the hat and the sign indicated that she had been convicted by a Church court.

She was taken first to the platform where her judges sat. One last time they faced each other—high-ranking churchmen, skilled lawyers, and learned professors on one side; the former simple peasant girl on the other. They had questioned her relentlessly for weeks during her Condemnation Trial, probing and prying, trying to trap her into an admission whereby they could brand her a witch. Her simple, straight-forward, innocent answers ruined their plans.

Joan had repeated to them what she had been saying to bishops, dukes, and even a king for two

Joan of Arc's execution took place in this marketplace in Rouen, France. Pictured is how the marketplace looked in the 1930s. In Joan's time, the buildings on either side of the photo extended to the sidewalk. The Church of St. Maclou, in the background, was built during the fifteenth and sixteenth centuries.

years—that she had been sent by God, through the voices of his saints, to deliver France from the English. She had led the French to unexpected victories. The English and Burgundians—who were Frenchmen but allies of the English—were afraid that she would so inspire her countrymen that they would drive out the English. Her enemies felt she had to be discredited and destroyed.

A week before the scene in the marketplace, a weary and frightened Joan had signed a paper promising, among other things, to stop wearing men's clothes, something her judges said was forbidden by the Bible and thus went against "God in His sacraments."[2] Three days later, Joan put on men's clothes again and said her voices had instructed her to do so. It was this that brought her to the stake.

A Final Prayer

Now, however, there were no more questions. Instead, a priest, Nicolas Midy, delivered a lengthy sermon as the English soldiers fidgeted. Afterward, Joan knelt to pray, calling on all present to pray for her and forgiving them for what they were about to do. The prayer was a long one, about half an hour. Many in the audience were in tears, but not all. One of the English soldiers called out to Jean Massieu, whose job it would be to comfort Joan as the fire was lit, "Priest, are you going to let us get done in time for dinner?"[3]

Finally, Pierre Cauchon, bishop of Beauvais and Joan's harshest judge, pronounced the sentence:

"We . . . cast you forth and reject you from the communion of the Church as an infected limb, and hand you over to secular justice."[4] But there would be no formal sentence from a secular, or non-Church, court. Joan was hustled from the platform and hauled before an official of Rouen, who simply made a gesture of dismissal with his hand.

As she was led to the stake, Joan cried out for a cross—a symbol of Christianity—to hold. An English soldier quickly bound two sticks together. Joan kissed the crude cross and placed it inside her dress, above her heart. Meanwhile, Massieu sent a fellow priest, Isambart de La Pierre, to fetch a crucifix—a cross with a representation of Jesus Christ on it—from a nearby church.

The Execution

Rough hands propelled Joan onto the third platform, to the stake. The executioner, Maugier Leparmentier, bound her with chains, since ropes would burn through. When she was secured, he climbed down, seized a waiting torch, and thrust it into the pile.

As Father Isambart held the cross aloft, where Joan could see it through the smoke, the flames leaped up around her. At least six times, Leparmentier later said, she called out "Jesus!" in a loud voice.[5] At last, her head fell forward. Joan of Arc was dead.

The marketplace was silent, except for the crackle of the flames and the sobbing of some of the onlookers. Few—even among the English—expressed

Joan of Arc grabs a cross held out by Father Isambert, as soldiers stack wood around the stake she is tied to.

any joy in what they had done. The executioner, having witnessed Joan's prayers and courage, said he was damned because he had put a holy person to death. One of the judges, Jean Alespée, said, "I wish that my soul were where I believe this woman's soul is."[6]

Another witness, John Tressart, a secretary to the king of England, cried out, "We are lost; we have burnt a saint."[7] Joan of Arc would, indeed, be proclaimed a saint, though it would take almost another five hundred years. Long before then, however, her spirit would burn in the hearts of the French as brightly as had the flames of Rouen. More than twenty years of warfare still lay ahead, but her dreams of a united and victorious France would come true.

Chapter 2

The Endless War

The war in which Joan of Arc gave her life had begun almost one hundred years before the events in the marketplace at Rouen. The conflict was not continuous, but rather ebbed and flowed, spreading misery over France like a tide. In the 1800s, French historians began calling it the *Guerre de Cent Ans*—the Hundred Years' War—even though it lasted 118 years, from 1337 to 1453.

The root causes of the war went back much farther—to 1066 when a daring French duke, William of Normandy, successfully invaded England and became king. This created a situation whereby William was king of England but yet owed allegiance to the king of France. This was possible under the social, economic, and military system known as feudalism.

The Feudal System

Under feudalism, members of the rich upper classes were granted lands by higher-ranking nobles in exchange for military service. Those who received the lands were called vassals. For one king to be the vassal of another would work only as long as the interests of the kings did not conflict. Such a conflict occurred about one hundred years after William's death. His great-grandson, Henry II—through inheritance and marriage—controlled much of France. This led to a bitter rivalry between Henry and the kings of France.

The tension reached a peak in 1328 when King Charles IV of France died. Only a male could succeed him, but Charles had no son. A council of nobles gave the throne to Charles's cousin, Philip of Valois, but there was another claimant—King Edward III of England.

Edward was the son of Isabella, an older sister of Charles IV. Edward was only fifteen years old at the time and lacked the military might to enforce his claim. Furthermore, the French did not want what they considered a foreign king, even though he was a French duke whose native language and culture were French.

Edward waited. He secretly aided France's enemies until Philip at last took action. On May 24, 1337, Philip declared that Edward, because of acts against the king, had forfeited any lands in France. Edward, in turn, sent a letter to Philip "who calls himself King of France," saying that he, Edward, was the rightful king.[1] The Hundred Years' War had begun.

The Battle of Sluys

The first battle of the war took place in 1340 at the French seaport of Sluys just above the English Channel between England and France, where Philip's fleet was anchored. (Today, Sluys is called "Sluis" and is located in southwest Netherlands, right near the Belgian border.) Edward knew that any further invasions of France would depend on control of the channel.

The Battle of Sluys was a complete victory for the English. The key difference between the two armies was that the English soldiers were armed with long-bows and the French with crossbows. The crossbow had a greater range and was more accurate, but the longbow could be fired more rapidly. A seasoned longbowman could fire five arrows for every one fired by a crossbowman.

Edward's opportunity for invasion came in 1346 when civil war broke out in Brittany, a large region on the western coast of France. With most of the French Army, commanded by Philip's son John, occupied there, Edward made a surprise landing in Normandy to the north on July 5. His army began marching toward Paris.

Philip advanced with an army that, despite the absence of those with Prince John, was far larger than Edward's. The English king, fearing he might be

Source Document

Since the kingdom of France has by divine disposition devolved [come] upon us by the clearest right owing to the death of Charles of noted memory, the last king of France, brother germane [having the same parents] to our lady mother, and the lord Philip of Valois, son of the king's uncle and thus farther removed in blood from the said king, and holds that kingdom against God and justice, lest we should seem to neglect our right and the gift of heavenly grace or to be unwilling to conform the impulse of our will to the divine pleasure, we have recognised our right to the kingdom and have undertaken the burden of the rule of that kingdom, as we ought to do, resolving with unshakable purpose to act with good and devoted servants, to do justice to all men according to the just and laudable customs of all men, to revive the good laws and customs which were in force in the time of Louis, our predecessor, and to cast out that usurper [Philip] when opportunity shall seem most propitious [favorable]. . . . Given at Ghent on the 8th of February, in the first year of our reign over France and the 14th of our rule over England.[2]

In 1340, partially in order to impress his allies, Edward III formally assumed the title of "King of France" by issuing this proclamation.

caught between the two French forces, began retreating north. Philip pursued rapidly and caught up with Edward near the village of Crécy.

Importance of Crécy

The Battle of Crécy resulted in another overwhelming English victory. Again, the longbow made the

Edward III's English force defeated Philip VI's French force at the Battle of Crécy on August 26, 1346.

difference. A deadly hail of arrows mowed down ranks of French knights and their horses before they could reach the English battle line. King Philip had to flee the battlefield to avoid capture.

Crécy was a turning point in warfare. The common soldier, armed with a longbow, had shown himself superior to the mounted, armored knight, long considered the ultimate military force. King Edward was hailed as the finest general in Europe, and the English were considered the best fighters. The disheartened French began to regard the English as invincible.

Two years after the Battle of Crécy, the war came to almost a complete standstill. A terrible and highly contagious sickness known as the Black Death reached Europe, having originated in China. It has been estimated that one-third of the population of Europe died. A monk wrote at the time that "the living were scarce able to bury the dead."[3]

In 1355, Edward resumed the war, sending an army commanded by his son Edward, known as the Black Prince because of the color of his armor. They marched through southern France, burning and stealing. John II, now king after his father Philip's death, raised an army to attack the Black Prince. The armies met near the city of Poitiers.

The Battle of Poitiers

The Battle of Poitiers between Prince Edward and King John in 1356 was almost a copy of the Battle of

Crécy fought between their fathers ten years earlier. Once more, the English archers cut down the French knights. King John was captured and sent to England as a prisoner. He was to be returned only on payment of a huge ransom.

France was in chaos. Groups of former soldiers—English, French, mercenaries from Germany and Italy—formed the so-called Free Companies, bandits who looted and terrorized the countryside. The French government was helpless.

King Edward launched another invasion in 1359, but a freak hailstorm killed many of his soldiers. Edward saw it as a warning from God and negotiated the Treaty of Brétigny with the French in 1360. King John's ransom was reduced. Edward agreed to drop his claim to the French throne in exchange for complete rule—not as a French vassal—over the region of Guyenne, in far southwestern France, and other territories.

These terms, called "renunciations," were signed but never formally exchanged. Finally, in 1363, Edward demanded that the French *Estates General,* or legislative body, approve the treaty. It was rejected. The fight against it was led by King John II's son and heir, Prince Charles, who was convinced the English could be defeated and led the fight against the treaty.

Charles the Wise

John II died in England the next year. The new French king, Charles V, is known to history as Charles the

Wise. He fought against the English his own way—not in great and glorious battles, which he likely would have lost, but with a long series of small skirmishes and political maneuvers. He gained control of Flanders, previously an English ally, when his brother, the duke of Burgundy (in western France), married the Flemish countess. This was a brilliant move at the time, but would have serious consequences for France later because it increased Burgundy's power.

Little by little, the territory gained by England slipped away. By 1374, almost everything the English had won in thirty-seven years of warfare had been lost. They might have been expelled from France altogether, but both sides were worn out.

The Black Prince died in 1376. His father, Edward III, died the next year, and King Charles V of France died in 1380. Both countries now had boy kings. The Black Prince's son, Richard II, was ten when crowned in 1377. The new king of France was twelve-year-old Charles VI.

Struggles for Control

Factions in each country fought for control of the young monarchs. Both France and England, therefore, had too many internal problems for their war against each other to continue. Although there would be brief raids, the Hundred Years' War would not be resumed in force for another thirty-five years.

Much happened, however, during this time. Richard II was overthrown in 1399 by his cousin,

Henry of Bolingbroke. The new King, Henry IV, favored a renewal of the war with France. However, he lacked money and had to contend with rebellions in Scotland and Wales.

Meanwhile, in France, young King Charles VI was controlled by a council dominated by his uncle, Philip the Bold, duke of Burgundy. Charles tried to gain his independence, dismissing his uncle and forming his own council. In 1392, however, he became insane. A struggle for power broke out between his uncle—Philip the Bold of Burgundy—and his cousin Louis, duke of Orléans.

The struggle divided France into two factions. The division grew deeper when Philip of Burgundy was succeeded as duke by his son, John the Fearless. John was even more ambitious than his father. The dukes of Burgundy and Orléans were bitter enemies. Finally, in 1407, John had Louis assassinated, and the feud became a civil war. The Burgundians were on one side and the Armagnacs on the other. The Armagnacs took their name from a count whose son had married Louis's daughter.

An Invitation

Fighting between the factions raged for years. Then in 1411—one year before the birth of Joan of Arc—John of Burgundy, desperate for aid, invited King Henry IV to send an army from England. John thus struck the spark that would rekindle the Hundred Years' War.

Soon, the Burgundians and the Armagnacs were both trying to get help from the English. Henry, however, was cautious. He sent only a small force to the aid of the Armagnacs. By the time it arrived, a truce had been called, but that did not stop the English from looting the countryside until they were bought off with a huge payment.

King Henry IV of England died in 1413 and was succeeded by his son, Henry V. This king was much bolder than his father, casting his eye—as had his great-grandfather Edward III—on the throne of France.

Henry landed an army in Normandy in August, 1415 intending to march on Paris. Instead, after some delays and with winter approaching and many of his men suffering from disease, he decided to retreat. The French—mostly the Armagnac faction, which had gained the upper hand in the civil war—pursued him and cornered him near the village of Agincourt on October 25, 1415.

Once again, an English force faced a much larger French army. The result was an English victory, much the same as at Crécy and Poitiers. Henry returned to England, wealthy with stolen goods. He easily raised the money and soldiers for a second, much larger invasion in 1417.

Meanwhile, the Armagnacs had lost many of their leading nobles at Agincourt. King Charles VI's two oldest sons had died, leaving his son Charles, a weak-charactered boy of fourteen, as dauphin—heir to the

King Henry V (left, in the foreground) defends his brother (left, on ground) against the French during the Battle of Agincourt on October 25, 1415. The English force of six thousand archers, one thousand cavalry soldiers, and a few thousand foot soldiers defeated a French force of twenty-five thousand.

French throne. Even Isabeau, the queen of France, considered her husband's cause lost and deserted him, joining John, duke of Burgundy.

Conquest of Normandy

Henry and his army had landed in August and began their conquest of Normandy. At about the same time, John of Burgundy surrounded Paris, hoping to capture it from the Armagnacs. The city surrendered in May 1418, but the dauphin escaped and took refuge in the south.

Paris was still in danger, however, from the approaching English army. The danger was so great that John of Burgundy opened negotiations with the remnants of the Armagnacs for a joint effort to rid France of the invaders.

In September 1419, John and the dauphin, with a few attendants each, met in the center of a bridge at Montereau. John proclaimed his willingness to make peace. The dauphin, however, signaled to one of his men, who leaped forward and killed the duke of Burgundy with an axe.

The Treaty of Troyes

With the assassination of John the Fearless, no agreement was possible. Indeed, John's successor as duke, Philip the Good, joined forces with the English. They drew up and signed the Treaty of Troyes in March 1420. Henry would marry Catherine, daughter of King Charles VI, and receive a huge dowry. (A dowry is money or property that a man receives from his wife in marriage.) At the same time, Philip's sister Anne was to marry King Henry's younger brother, the duke of Bedford. Charles VI would remain king, but Henry would succeed him. The dauphin was disinherited by Queen Isabeau, who suddenly claimed that King Charles was not her son's real father.

Henry and his new queen, Catherine, departed for England early in 1421. Soon afterward, the forces loyal to Charles, the dauphin, rallied. Henry hurried back to France, leaving a pregnant Catherine behind. His military campaign was successful. The dauphin was forced once more to flee south to the area of France loyal to him. Henry, however, fell ill and died on September 1, 1422. He was thirty-five years old. The new king of England was the infant Henry VI, who had been born to Catherine the previous December.

Two months later, King Charles VI of France also died. According to the Treaty of Troyes, Henry VI—still less than a year old—became King Henri II of France. Two royal uncles—the duke of Gloucester in England and the duke of Bedford in France—would act as regents, ruling in the young king's name.

A Divided France

France was thus split into four areas. The English ruled Normandy and Brittany. The duke of Burgundy ruled in Flanders as well as Burgundy. The remaining area north of the Loire River, including Paris, was controlled jointly by Bedford and Philip the Good. The huge territory south of the Loire—except for Guyenne, which was still English—remained loyal to the dauphin.

In 1427, Bedford decided on a major campaign in the south designed to end the war. He needed a base for his operations and picked Orléans, which stood on the Loire as the gateway to southern France, stronghold of the dauphin.

The siege of Orléans began on October 1, 1428, with the earl of Salisbury commanding the English. The dauphin appealed to Philip of Burgundy, as a fellow Frenchman, to help. But Philip remembered the murder of his father. All he would do was remove a small number of Burgundian troops who were with the English.

Both sides thought that the fall of Orléans would mean the end of the dauphin's cause. The war that had raged for almost one hundred years appeared to be headed toward conclusion. Only a miracle, it seemed, could save France. That miracle appeared on the scene in the person of Joan of Arc.

Domrémy

By 1428, the Hundred Years' War seemed to be drawing to a close. France was on the brink of final and complete defeat by the English and Burgundians. Charles, the disinherited dauphin, showed neither the desire nor the ability to regain his kingdom. In the end, France would not be saved by any dauphin, duke, or mighty warrior, but by a poor peasant girl—Joan of Arc. But, before she could overcome the English, she would have to overcome the doubts of those she said God had sent her to help.

Domrémy lay on the western bank of the Meuse River in eastern France. It was far removed from the greatest battles of the war but was no stranger to conflict. Domrémy was a border town, partially in France and partially in the nearby dukedom of Bar, loyal to the duke of Burgundy. As in much of France,

Joan of Arc was born in the French village of Domrémy. Today the village is called Domrémy-la-Pucelle, and the house where Joan was born is a museum.

occasional raids had become a part of life for the villagers, much like droughts or floods.

Joan's Family

It was here in Domrémy, probably on January 6, 1412, that Joan was born. Her father was Jacques d'Arc, a moderately prosperous farmer and a man of some standing in the community. Her mother was Isabelle Romeé, a woman known for her religious character.

Joan, called Jeanette by everyone in Domrémy, was one of five children born to the d'Arcs. She had two older brothers, Jacquemin and Jean; a younger brother, Pierre; and one sister, Catherine, thought to have died young. The children worked hard, as did everyone in the village. There were crops to be tended, livestock to care for, and wood to chop.

Such work required a strong body. Later descriptions of Joan show her to have been a typical French peasant woman—short, dark, and sturdily built—strong enough to ride a warhorse and to wield a sword or a lance. She was feminine but was far from the willowy blonde figure sometimes portrayed by later artists.

Exceptional Devotion

Joan took her turn with the rest of the children, driving cattle to the fields and keeping watch over them. Whenever she could, however, she slipped away from this task and walked through the nearby forest to a tiny chapel dedicated to the Virgin Mary. (In the Catholic religion, the Virgin Mary is the mother of Jesus Christ.) There, Joan would pray until she had to return to work.

Joan was very religious. Long after her death, some of her friends remembered teasing her because she would kneel in the fields to pray when she heard church bells. She loved the sound of the bells, and would even take little cakes to the village bell ringer.

The people of Domrémy were fiercely loyal to the dauphin. Boys and young men sometimes fought those from the neighboring village of Maxey, which was Burgundian. Joan was just as patriotic as the rest, if not more so. There was only one person in Domrémy who openly sided with the Burgundians. Joan later said she would have been glad to see his head cut off, "if that had been God's pleasure."[1]

Joan's Voices

Joan's life changed forever in the summer of 1424. As described at her trial, "... from the age of thirteen, she received revelation from Our Lord by a voice which taught her how to behave. And the first time she was greatly afraid."[2]

Initially, Joan said, the voice told her only that it had been sent by God, who expected great things of her. She was instructed to go to church often and to lead a pure life, remaining a virgin—never having sexual relations with a man. If she did this, God would protect her. She told no one—neither parents nor priest—about the voice. She heard the voice again days later, and then again. By the third time, she said, she was no longer afraid. She knew it was "the voice of an angel," which later identified itself to her as Saint Michael the Archangel.[3]

Later, she heard other voices, which Saint Michael identified to her as Saint Catherine and Saint Margaret, two of Joan's favorite saints. In time, the voices became more real to Joan. She said that she was able to see, touch, and even smell these heavenly apparitions. She claimed she frequently was able to see other angels, but the only voices she heard were of these three.

Historians and clergymen have speculated for centuries about Joan's "voices." Were they truly saints

Source Document

I was thirteen when I had a Voice from God for my help and guidance. The first time that I heard this Voice, I was very much frightened; it was mid-day, in the summer, in my father's garden. I had not fasted the day before. I heard this Voice to my right, towards the Church; rarely do I hear it without its being accompanied also by a light. This light comes from the same side [as] the Voice. Generally, it is a great light. . . . If I were in a wood, I could easily hear the Voice when [it] came to me. It seemed to me to come from lips I should reverence. I believe it was sent me from God. When I heard it for the third time, I recognized that it was the Voice of an Angel. . . . It said to me two or three times a week: "You must go into France. . . . Go, raise the siege which is being made before the City of Orléans."[4]

At her Condemnation Trial at Rouen, Joan gave this account of the first time she heard her "voices" in Domrémy.

sent by God, who had chosen this girl as his tool? Or were they only the imaginings of an impressionable child? There is no firm answer. Most writers agree with author Kelly DeVries that the reality of the visions is beside the point, that what is important "is that *she* believed they came from God."[5] Joan was convinced that they were real. Her belief gave her the courage and confidence to carry out the mission she believed she was given.

Joan's Mission

The voices did not rush Joan or overwhelm her about the task ahead. Bit by bit, they revealed her mission to her. First, she was told only that she would have to travel into France to aid the dauphin. In 1428, however, the voices grew specific. Joan was to go to the nearby fortress town of Valcouleurs. There, she was to convince its captain, Robert de Baudricourt, to send her to the dauphin at Chinon. From Chinon, she was to lead troops to lift the English siege of Orléans, after which she would escort the dauphin to Reims (modern-day spelling), where he would be crowned king.

Later, at her trial, Joan said that she wept and protested that she was "only a poor woman, who knew nothing of riding [horses] or of making war."[6] The voices said she should take a standard, or banner, "in the Name of the King of Heaven."[7] Under this standard she would win all battles she fought and be under God's protection.

This is an artist's interpretation of Joan listening to her voices. This painting by L. F. Benouville hangs in the Museum of Reims.

Joan turned for help to an older cousin by marriage, Durand Lassois, who lived near Valcouleurs. In May 1428, she went to visit Lassois and told him what she must do, asking him to take her to Baudricourt.

Dismissal

Lassois reluctantly agreed and escorted Joan, in her red peasant woman's dress, to the castle. According to Bertrand de Poulengy, an eyewitness, Joan first told Baudricourt he should send a message to Charles, the dauphin, to refrain from battle. She said God would soon send him help. She said the kingdom of France was not the dauphin's concern but that of her Lord. When Baudricourt asked who she meant by her "Lord," she answered, "The King of Heaven."[8] God intended Charles to be king, she added, and she herself would lead him to be crowned.

Baudricourt, a battle-hardened veteran, threw back his head and laughed. He told Lassois to take Joan back to her father and advise him to give her a good beating. He jokingly threatened that if she returned he would turn her over to his soldiers as a plaything. Disappointed, but not discouraged, Joan returned to Domrémy.

Return to Valcouleurs

In January 1429, Joan's voices insisted that she go once more to Valcouleurs. She told friends she was going to help Lassois's wife, who was expecting a baby. She told her parents nothing, simply packing her few belongings and slipping out of the house. She called good-byes to those she passed on her way out of the village. She would never see Domrémy again. She was barely seventeen years old.

Joan remained in Valcouleurs for six weeks, spending some of the time with Lassois and some in the home of Catherine and Henri de Royer. Her reception by Baudricourt was very different from before. The war was not going well. Also, two of his officers—Bertrand de Poulengy and Jean de Metz—had taken up her cause. Poulengy had been present at the first meeting. Metz, curious about Joan, met her at the Royer house, heard her story, and pledged to help her. It was Metz, thinking about the dangers she might encounter on the journey, who first suggested that Joan wear men's clothing. She agreed, and he gave her clothes and boots belonging to one of his servants.

She met Baudricourt again, demanding to be given an escort to Chinon. He refused and sent her away, but not as rudely as before. It was a religious age, and many more people than today—even rough soldiers— believed in miracles. Perhaps this peasant girl could somehow help. Baudricourt sent a messenger to Chinon, asking permission to send Joan to the dauphin.

Passing a Test

In the meantime, however, Baudricourt wanted to assure himself that she had been sent by God and

Joan of Arc embarked on a religious mission at the age of seventeen. Throughout her journey, her faith would be tested many times by skeptics and the extreme hardships she would endure.

not the devil. He went to the Royer house with a priest, Jean Fournier, and asked to see Joan. Catherine de Royer later testified that Joan told her that the priest said he was wearing a garment that had been blessed. If Joan were a witch, he said, she could not approach, but if she were good, she had nothing to fear. As Catherine testified: "Then [Joan] drew near the Priest and threw herself at his knees: she said he was wrong to act so, for he had heard her in confession."[9]

Still, Baudricourt would not send her to Chinon, having received no reply to his message. Joan grew impatient. To her, the mission was obvious. She could not understand why Baudricourt hesitated.

Joan confronted Baudricourt on February 12. She said the dauphin had suffered a defeat and that worse would happen if Baudricourt did not send her to Chinon. Shortly thereafter, a messenger arrived with news that Charles's forces had indeed been defeated at Rouvroay a few days before. Joan could not possibly have known this in advance.

This apparent miracle was enough for Baudricourt. In addition, another messenger, Colet de Vienne, arrived from Chinon. He carried a letter from the dauphin allowing Joan to come to him.

On February 23, the small party set out from Valcouleurs. It was to be a long journey—three hundred fifty miles—through dangerous territory. For safety's sake, Joan not only dressed in men's clothing, but also cut her hair short. She was accompanied only by Poulengy and Metz, two of their servants, Vienne, and an archer named Richard. As they rode forth, Baudricourt, probably glad to see the last of her, said, "Go, go, let come what may."[10] Joan of Arc had cleared her first obstacle. Many more lay in her path.

Chinon

Joan of Arc set out for Chinon riding a borrowed horse, wearing cast-off men's clothes, and traveling with only six companions. This peasant girl—speaking plainly and boldly, sure of her mission—was out to convince the great nobles of France that she had been sent to save their country.

The journey took eleven days. Sometimes the little group sought shelter in a church. Some nights they slept on the ground, Metz and Poulengy sleeping on either side of Joan. It was possible that they did not altogether trust Colet de Vienne. Perhaps they had heard that some of the dauphin's advisers had been opposed to her visit.

Joan's only complaint was that they did not stop often enough to attend mass at the churches they passed. She would have preferred to stop every day, sometimes more than once. In the end, they attended mass only twice, at Auxerre and at Fierbois. The second stop was highly significant for Joan because the church was dedicated to Saint Catherine, whom she had identified as one of her voices.

"La Pucelle"

At Fierbois, Joan dictated a letter to be sent ahead to the dauphin. She said she had traveled to come to his aid and that she knew many things that would be of benefit to him. Also, she wrote she would be able to recognize him even though they had never met. In the letter, she referred to herself as *Jehanne la Pucelle,* Joan the Maid.

The choice of the word *pucelle* was important. It means "virgin" rather than merely "young girl." The significance is that, according to the beliefs of the time, the devil could not work through a virgin. Joan was thus telling Charles that she was a pure instrument of God. She said later that her voices had called her *La Pucelle,* and it would be by that name that she would become famous.

Joan entered Chinon on Sunday, March 6, 1429, and waited on word from Charles. It was not until after supper on Tuesday, however, that she was ushered into the great hall of Chinon. Light blazed from dozens of torches. The hall was crowded with noble lords and ladies curious to see her, even if few probably believed she was what she claimed to be.

Joan arrives at Chinon Castle, hoping to speak with the dauphin. The castle still stands today and is 1,300 feet long and 230 feet wide.

Their splendid garments contrasted oddly with the shabby men's clothes she still wore.

Another Test

Charles was skeptical and had a test for Joan. His clothes were nowhere near as rich as some worn by those around him. He was not standing in the center of the hall, nor seated on a throne, but instead was off to one side among a group. Joan was not fooled. She went immediately to Charles, knelt, and said, "Gentle dauphin, I am Joan the Maid. The King of Heaven sends me to you with the message that you shall be anointed and crowned in the city of Reims, and that you shall be the lieutenant of the King of Heaven, who is the King of France."[1]

Charles still was not convinced. He told Joan she was mistaken and pointed to a richly dressed noble, saying he was the dauphin. Joan was firm. "In God's name, sweet Prince, it is you and none other."[2]

The Dauphin

There was certainly little that was regal about Charles. When he met Joan, he was twenty-six years old, thin and frail, with skinny legs and knobby knees. Portraits show thick lips, watery eyes without lashes, and a long, bulbous nose. Behind his back, people called him *Le Falot,* meaning "the dreary."

His dress was just as dreary as his appearance. He had fled from Paris when it was taken by the English in 1420 and had spent the last eight years wandering from castle to castle. He found hospitality and borrowed money wherever he could, even from his cook at one point.

None of this mattered to Joan. To her, Charles was

In this engraving by J. Park, Charles is depicted as he looked as dauphin.

only her *gentil Dauphin,* chosen—as she had been—by God. Perhaps her simple answer had communicated this, because the prince raised her to her feet and led her aside so they could talk privately. After a few moments, Joan was dismissed. Charles's courtiers, or members of his royal court, could see that his face, normally gloomy, was joyful. Joan's priest at Chinon, Jean Pasquerel, said that the dauphin "said to his courtiers that Joan had told him a certain secret that no one knew or could know except God; and that is why he had great confidence in her."[3]

Historians have wondered for centuries about Joan's so-called "king's secret." It probably had to do with the single issue at the heart of Charles's doubts and fears: his birth. Joan may have told him that God had assured her that Charles was the true ruler of France.

Alençon and La Trémoïlle

Still, Charles had to make sure that Joan was a true messenger of God. Joan was given rooms in the palace, complete with a private chapel, and her own page, or attendant. She continued to be questioned. She was even examined physically to ensure that she was female. She had long discussions with the dauphin, his adviser and favorite Georges de La Trémoïlle, and the duke of Alençon.

These two men were completely different from one another and in their outlook toward Joan. La Trémoïlle, eighteen years older than Charles, had a big influence over the dauphin, who owed him huge sums of money. He was jealous of anyone who threatened his control of Charles and thus resented Joan's presence.

Alençon was twenty-three, only six years older than Joan, and he became fast friends with her. They went riding together, and Joan was so skilled at tilting—wielding a lance on horseback—that he gave her a black horse as a present.

Poitiers

Charles, however, had lingering doubts about Joan. He wanted her examined at Poitiers, about fifty miles south of Chinon, where some scholars from the University of Paris had taken refuge. Charles himself went with her. Joan apparently had no idea where she was being taken. On being told halfway through the journey, she said, "I know I shall have a lot of trouble at Poitiers, but *messires* [her voices] will help me; so let us go."[4]

At Poitiers, Joan was questioned by some of the most learned men in France, led by Regnault of Chartres, the dauphin's chancellor, or chief minister, who was also the archbishop of Reims. Whether aided by her voices or not, she more than stood her ground, answering openly and courageously. One of her questioners said, "This girl spoke terribly well. I would really like to have had so fine a daughter."[5]

Joan of Arc was not the same girl who earlier had wept in terror at the thought of leading an army.

Source Document

I, in my turn, asked Jeanne what dialect the Voice spoke? "A better one than yours," she replied. I speak the Limousin dialect. "Do you believe in God?" I asked her. "In truth, more than yourself!" she answered. "But God wills that you should not be believed unless there appear some sign to prove that you ought to be believed; and we shall not advise the King to trust in you, and to risk an army on your simple statement." "In God's Name!" she replied, "I am not come to Poitiers to show signs: but send me to Orléans, where I shall show you the signs by which I am sent": and she added: "Send me men in such numbers as may seem good, and I will go to Orléans."[6]

Joan's courage before her questioners at Poitiers is demonstrated in this later account by Brother Seguin de Seguin.

Everything had unfolded just as her voices said they would. She had convinced Baudricourt; she had convinced the dauphin. Now, she thought, it was time for action. She once again grew impatient. Urged to show some sign that she had, indeed, been sent by God, she said, "I am not come to Poitiers to show signs: but send me to Orleans, where I shall show you the signs by which I am sent."[7]

At Poitiers, Joan was questioned by scholars who were loyal to Charles, the dauphin. After hearing from a determined Joan, the scholars were convinced that she should proceed with her mission to Orléans.

Finally, her questioners were convinced. One later said, "We reported all this to the Council of the King; and we were of opinion that, considering the extreme necessity and the great peril of the town, the King might make use of her help and send her to Orleans."[8]

Letter to the Enemy

Before leaving Poitiers for Chinon, Joan dictated a letter—since she could neither read nor write—to the English that shows the extent of her confidence. It would have been a very bold letter for anyone, even the dauphin himself, to have written. For a seventeen-year-old girl to have done so is clear evidence that she thought she spoke with the voice of God:

> Jhesus Maria. King of England, and you, Duke of Bedford, calling yourself Regent of France; William de la Pole, Earl of Suffolk; John Lord Talbot, and you, Thomas Lord Scales, calling yourselves lieutenants of the said Bedford . . . deliver the keys of all the good towns you have taken and violated in France to the Maid who has been sent by God the King of Heaven. . . . Go away, for God's sake, back to your own country; otherwise, await news of the Maid, who will soon visit you to your great detriment [harm].[9]

Joan was to lead an army to Orléans, but the needy dauphin had no army at hand. While Alençon took charge of assembling soldiers, weapons, and provisions at Blois, midway between Chinon and Orléans, Joan was sent to Tours. There she was fitted for a suit of armor, not as thick as would have been worn by a man but still heavy enough that only a sturdily built woman could have worn it comfortably.

Sword and Banner

Joan was offered a sword and surprised everyone by asking that a messenger be sent to Fierbois, to the Church of Saint Catherine where she had stopped on her way from Valcouleurs. Buried behind the altar, she said, would be the sword she wanted. The sword, which no one at the church had known about, was unearthed, cleaned, and brought to Blois, to which Joan had moved to join the army.

Finally, she asked that a banner be made for her to carry to Orléans. Later, she would say that her voices were very specific as to what the banner would depict: the world, supported by two angels; a portrait of Jesus; the lilies symbolic of France; and the words *Jhesus Maria,* all painted on white fringed with silk. She usually preferred carrying the banner to carrying a sword. When asked why, she said, "Because I do not wish to use my sword, nor to kill any one."[10]

Joan of Arc said that the design of her banner was dictated by the voices she heard.

*Joan receives the sword she said would be found on the grounds of
the Church of Saint Catherine in Fierbois, France.*

Thus equipped, Joan set out in mid-April 1429. She tried to mount her horse, the same one that she had been given by Alençon. The horse shied away. "Lead him to the cross," she said.[11] The horse was led to a nearby church with a large cross on the door and immediately became quiet and docile. Joan swung up into the saddle and led the army out of the city. Ahead lay Orléans and the destiny of France.

Chapter 5

Orléans

Inspired and led by Joan of Arc, the French would lift a siege that had dragged on for eight months in only nine days. The strategic importance of Orléans, however, was secondary. What was important was that the French would finally win a victory, one that would lead to others. As one of Joan's biographers wrote, her "real achievement was not the relief of Orléans, but the regeneration of the soul of a flagging [weak and spiritless] France."[1]

Orléans, in fact, did not fit the usual picture of a medieval siege. The French were not so weak, nor the English so strong, as sometimes supposed. The English, commanded by Sir John Talbot, had endured a hard winter, losing many men to disease. Furthermore, Philip of Burgundy had withdrawn his troops, perhaps reluctant to besiege fellow

Frenchmen. Also, some of the Norman troops allied with England had grown weary and returned home.

Orléans

Orléans, a city of about thirty thousand, lay on the north bank of the Loire River, about thirty-five miles east of Blois. The commander was John, count of Dunois, known as the Bastard of Orléans because he was the illegitimate (born out of wedlock) son of the duke of Orléans. The duke had been killed by John of Burgundy in 1407. The people lived within the strong city wall, which was four feet thick and from eighteen to thirty feet high. The wall was surrounded on the south by the river and on other sides by deep man-made bodies of water called moats.

The English were too few, and Orléans was too strong for it to be taken by assault. The English also could not completely surround the city, instead they circled it with eleven bastilles, or forts. Gaps two to three miles wide existed between the bastilles, however, which allowed men and provisions to slip in.

The French army, with its load of provisions for Orléans, left Blois on April 17. The strategy was to march along the south bank of the Loire to a spot east of Orléans opposite the village of Chéchy, then float the convoy back downriver and enter the city from the least-defended side. The plan was sound, but there was one problem. Those who devised it did not inform Joan.

51

Although the dauphin had said, "Nothing shall be done without reference to the Maid, no matter how many good and competent men of war there may be present," his orders were ignored.[2] Joan was not in command. Instead, the army was led by Saint-Sévère de Boussac and Gilles de Rais. Also holding high office was Etienne de Vignolles, known as *La Hire,* or "the Angry," who would play a major part in the battles to come.

Joan's Anger

Supremely confident, Joan expected to march straight to the gates of Orléans. When the army passed by Orléans to the south, the church spires of the city in sight, she knew she had been misled. Dunois, eager to meet this girl about whom he had heard so much, came across the river at Chéchy and met a rude reception instead. "Is it you who advised them to bring me here by this bank of the river, instead of sending me straight to Talbot and the English?" she demanded. "In God's name! the counsel of Our Lord is wiser and better than yours. You thought to deceive me, but you have deceived yourselves."[3]

It did, indeed, appear as if the soldiers' plan had backfired. The wind was from the west, making it impossible for the barges to sail in that direction. Joan told them to be patient. Suddenly, the wind changed, and the barges were loaded.

Joan and Dunois then disagreed about whether the army would proceed to Orléans. Dunois and the other officers thought there were not enough men to lift the siege. They wanted the army to return to Blois, get reinforcements, then march back. Dunois, however, did want Joan to accompany him into the city, where she was eagerly awaited.

Entry Into Orléans

Joan hesitated, not wanting to be separated from the army, but at last consented. The army marched back the way it came. The barges went downriver. Joan and Dunois rode toward Orléans, entering the city around dusk. She rode a white horse, having exchanged the one given to her by Alençon. A crowd of people lined the streets to see La Pucelle, this maid who was to be their savior.

Joan spent most of the next day, Saturday, April 30, 1429, in discussions with Dunois and his officers. Not everyone was ready to listen to her. Jean de Gamache protested at having to take "the advice of a little saucebox of low birth [smart aleck of humble origin]." He vowed to become a simple squire, rather than a knight, before he would serve under "a hussy [a lewd or overly bold woman] who once may have been God knows what."[4]

That same day, Joan sent a letter to the English, demanding their surrender. She also went to the north shore of the river facing the bastille known as *Les Tourelles.* She shouted to the commander, Sir William Gladsdale, repeating her demands. Gladsdale shouted back, calling Joan names, adding that the English would burn her if they captured her.

The next day, Dunois left with a small force for Blois to make sure the army returned. Joan and La Hire escorted them part of the way to prevent the English from attacking. Why the English did not attack Joan as she was riding back to Orléans, with Dunois gone, remains a mystery.

Tuesday and Wednesday, May 2 and 3, were relatively quiet. Many of the outlying towns, which had gotten word of Joan and her mission, sent soldiers to Orléans. At dawn on May 4, lookouts could see the French army heading back from Blois. Joan rode out with about five hundred men to meet them and escorted them back into the city.

Early that afternoon, Dunois came to Joan with news that the English officer Sir John Fastolf was on his way with reinforcements for Talbot. Joan was determined to attack before these new troops were in place. "Bastard, Bastard," she said, "in the name of God I command you that as soon as you hear of Fastolf's coming you will let me know. For, if he gets through without my knowing it, I swear to you that I will have your head cut off."[5]

First Taste of War

Shortly afterward, Joan lay down for a rest. With her was a squire, Jean d'Aulon, who said later that he was half asleep when Joan sprang up. "My voices have told me that I must go against the English," she cried. "The

Joan said that sometimes her voices spoke to her in her sleep. In this painting by George W. Joy, an angel watches over Joan as she slumbers.

blood of our people is running out upon the ground. . . . Why was I not roused earlier?"[6]

Hurriedly she put on her armor and rushed to the Burgundy Gate. An attack had been launched against the Bastille de Saint Loup on the north shore of the river to the east of Orléans. It is doubtful that Joan was not told of the attack. More likely it had taken place earlier than she expected.

The attack was not going well, but when the French saw Joan, they rallied, renewed the attack, and captured the bastille, or prison. It was an important victory. Not only was it the first bastille captured by the French, but it opened the way for supplies to be brought in from the east.

Perhaps shocked by her first sight of warfare, Joan ordered that there be no fighting the next day. Instead, the generals spent the day planning an attack on the Bastille de Saint Laurent to the west. Joan was not present, and the soldiers decided to tell her only part of the plan. When they did, Joan looked at them coldly and said, "Tell me what you have really decided."[7] Dunois and the rest were learning that it was hard to deceive someone who heard the voices of saints.

Another Message

Although she had decreed that there would be no fighting, Joan sent yet another message to the English, calling on them to surrender and warning that "if you do not so I shall make such a *hahay* [uproar] that will be perpetually remembered."[8] The letter was tied to an arrow and shot into the English camp. The English picked it up and shouted insults at Joan.[9] She burst into tears.

There was more fighting on the next day, Friday, May 6. The French attacked one of the smaller English forts, the Bastille de Saint Jean-le-Blanc, located on the south bank of the river to the east of the city. Seeing the size of the advancing force, the English abandoned the fort. They took refuge in the larger Bastille des Augustines located at the end of the bridge across the Loire.

Once again, Joan was late in arriving. The French had decided that they lacked the force to capture the Bastille des Augustines and were about to return to the city. At that point, Joan rode up with La Hire just as the English charged out of the bastille at the retreating French. "In the Lord's name, let us charge these English," Joan shouted.[10] She and La Hire, alone, rode forward. At their example, the French followed. Dunois appeared with fresh troops, and the bastille was captured. The French now controlled the entire south shore of the river. The English in the Bastille des Tourelles, on an island in the river, were now trapped.

A Prediction

Dunois and his captains hesitated to make a final attack. They told Joan they should wait on more reinforcements, but she had been listening to her voices. The assault would begin the next day, she told them. Then, speaking to her priest, Joan warned him to stay close to her the next day because "I shall have much to do, more than I ever had yet, and the blood will flow from my body above my breast."[11]

The Bastille des Tourelles, on an island in the Loire, was the most inaccessible of the English forts. The bridge to the north of the island, leading to the city, had been partially destroyed. A drawbridge to the south connected the fort with a large earth barricade, or protective wall. In front of the barricade was a deep ditch.

The French attacked across the ditch at dawn on May 7, throwing ladders against the side of the barricade. Time after time, they were thrown back. Arrows and stones rained down on them. At one point, thinking the French were on the point of retreating, Joan seized a ladder and flung it against the barricade. No sooner had she started to climb than an arrow from an English crossbow struck her in the shoulder, above the collarbone, penetrating clean through to the other side.

Instantly someone was at her side, helping her to rise. It was Jean de Gamache, the same knight who had vowed never to serve under a "saucebox." He prevented the English from climbing down to capture her, and gave her his horse, on which she was led from the battlefield.

Quick Return

Joan did not remain away for long. When the iron tip of the arrow had been cut off, she pulled the shaft out with her own hands. After the wound had been bandaged, she returned to the battle. By now it was almost night, and Dunois was ready to call for a retreat. Joan convinced him to delay, that all would be well. She withdrew to a nearby field to pray.

Joan's banner had been given to a soldier called "the Basque" to hold. Her squire, Jean d'Aulon, took it on himself to use it to rally the French. He told the Basque to follow him across the ditch in yet another charge, thinking that the sight of the banner would encourage the French.

D'Aulon charged, but the Basque did not follow. Joan had caught sight of her banner and, thinking it was about to be stolen, tried to take it from the Basque.

Joan of Arc was struck in the shoulder by an arrow as she climbed an English barricade. Though she was taken from the battlefield to have her wound treated, she would not stay away for long.

The waving of Joan's banner inspired the French to furiously attack the English, who were laying siege to the town of Orléans.

As they grappled for it, it waved to and fro. Dunois, thinking that this was a signal from Joan, mounted a charge so furious that the barricade was taken.

The Fall of the Bastille des Tourelles

Now, only the bastille itself was left. To the north, the people of Orléans rushed out of the gate and began to span the gap in the bridge with ladders and planks nailed together. Across this fragile walkway, they charged the English. Gladsdale and his remaining warriors, in a panic, ran south, through the fort and toward the drawbridge. But the French had rowed a flaming boat under the bridge, and some of the supporting timbers had burned away.

Joan cried out to the English captain, "Yield yourself to the King of Heaven! . . . You called me [an insulting name]. . . . Great pity do I feel for your soul."[12] It was too late. The bridge collapsed. Gladsdale and many others fell into the Loire and, weighted down by their armor, were drowned.

Talbot had had enough. The next day, Sunday, May 8, the English fell into formation, as if readying for battle. Instead, they marched away. The siege was over. Talbot would write to his king, Henry VI, that "a great mischief, sent, it seems to me, by the hand of God, fell upon your soldiers" caused by "that limb of Satan, named the Pucelle, who made use against them of false enchantments and sorcery."[13]

The people of Orléans celebrated, rich and poor mingling happily in a way seldom seen in those

Source Document

...Jeanne went out to the soldiers; and then she was asked, if it were well to fight against the English on that day, being Sunday; to which she answered that she must hear Mass [religious service]; whereupon she sent to fetch a table, and had the ornaments of the Church brought, and two Masses were celebrated, which she and the whole army heard with great devotion. Mass being ended, Jeanne asked if the English had their faces turned toward us; she was told no, that their faces were turned towards Meung. Hearing this, she said: "In God's Name, they are going; let them depart; and let us give thanks to God and pursue them no further, because it is Sunday."[14]

At Joan's Nullification Trial, Jean de Champeaux, a citizen of Orléans, explained how the English abandoned their siege.

class-conscious times. They pleaded with Joan to remain with them, but she was already looking to the future. She had been impatient with Dunois and the other soldiers because, to her, the lifting of the siege was only one part of her mission. The more important part was still to come, the ultimate goal given by her voices—the crowning of the dauphin in Reims.

Reims

After the victory at Orléans, Joan of Arc turned to her second great task, the coronation, or crowning, of the dauphin at Reims. As before, she faced heavy odds. This time, however, her enemies were not so much the English, as the hostility of Charles's advisers and the shyness of the prince himself.

Orléans greeted the departure of the English with an outpouring of joy and relief. People crowded around Joan, eager even to touch her clothing. She, however, wanted to move on. She did so the next day, after a service of thanksgiving, saying she "must needs go to the King with the good news, and urge him to set out for his coronation and anointing at Rheims."[1]

Charles Hesitates

This would be much easier said than done. The relief of Orléans had required neither action nor risk by

Charles, a man who disliked both. Had Joan failed, he would not have been much worse off than before. What Joan proposed now was different. He would have to go more than two hundred miles into Anglo-Burgundian territory.

Charles worried about failure. His advisers, La Trémoïlle and Regnault of Chartres, worried about success. They were extremely protective of their control over the dauphin. They had allowed him to let Joan to go to Orléans, probably thinking they had little to fear. If she succeeded in having him crowned, however, her influence might be greater than theirs.

Joan learned that Charles, who had remained in Chinon throughout the siege, was headed to Tours. She went there to meet him and, on May 13, rode out as he approached. As she bowed low before him, he took her hands, lifting her to her feet. An onlooker later said he looked so joyful "that he might have hugged her."[2] It was his only recorded public expression of affection or gratitude.

Joan begged him to go with her to Reims. He would not give her an answer. His councilors were raising all sorts of objections. Charles listened to all their arguments, but he also listened to Joan. She held before him the vision of himself anointed with holy oil and crowned, as had been his ancestors, in the great cathedral at Reims. It was a powerful argument for Charles, hounded for years about his right to be king of France.

Joan's Plea

The telling moment came when Joan entered a room where Charles was meeting with some of his councilors. Neither La Trémoïlle nor Regnault were present. Joan threw herself before the dauphin, embraced his knees, and said, "Noble Dauphin! hold no longer these many and long councils, but come quickly to Reims to take the crown for which you are worthy!" Asked if her voices had urged this, Joan answered that they had and had also said to her, "Daughter of God! go on! go on! go on! I will be thy Help: go on!"[3] Charles was finally convinced. He would go to Reims.

First, however, some English strongholds on the Loire had to be conquered. Even in her impatience, Joan had to agree. It would have been foolhardy to march into enemy territory leaving strong enemy forces to the rear. Accordingly, an army was formed under Alençon. It set out on June 10, 1429, with Joan carrying her banner.

The first objective was Jargeau, about fifteen miles upriver from Orléans. Alençon and his captains at first thought it was too strong to be taken, but Joan said God would aid them. "If I were not sure that it is God Who guides us," she scolded, "I would rather take care of the sheep than expose myself to such great perils."[4]

Encouraged by Joan, the French captured the town. More than eleven hundred Englishmen were

Source Document

"Forward, gentle Duke, to the assault," cried Jeanne to me. And when I told her it was premature to attack so quickly: "Have no fear," she said to me, "it is the right time when it pleases God; we must work when it is His Will: act, and God will act!" "Ah, gentle Duke," she said to me later, "are you afraid? Did you not know that I promised your wife to bring thee back, safe and sound? And indeed when I left my wife to come with Jeanne to the head-quarters of the army, my wife had told me that she feared much for me, that I had but just left prison [in England] and much had been spent on my ransom, and she would gladly have asked that I might remain with her. To this Jeanne had replied, "Lady, have no fear; I will give him back to you whole, or even in better case than he is now."[5]

The duke of Alençon needed some encouragement from Joan before the attack on the city of Jargeau was launched, as he testified at the Nullification Trial.

killed, and Michael de La Pole, earl of Suffolk, was made prisoner. One account, never confirmed, said he surrendered personally to Joan, calling her "the bravest woman in the world."[6]

A Premonition

Leaving the army in charge of the city, Joan and Alençon rode back to Orléans. As soon as she could, however, she hastened back to the army. Her voices had told her that time was limited. A week before, she had told Charles, "I shall last but little more than a year."[7]

The next target was Meung, beyond which was the far larger and stronger town of Beaugency, where Talbot had led the surviving English from Orléans. When the English retreated into the castle at Meung, the French simply moved on another five miles to Beaugency, leaving troops to keep the English bottled up.

Talbot had left the command of Beaugency to others and had headed north in search of Sir John Fastolf, who finally had arrived in the area after a delay of weeks. The troops Talbot left behind were not eager to fight and retreated behind the city walls, allowing the French to occupy the outskirts of the town.

Richemont

Just as this was being done, two messengers rode up, saying that an army led by Arthur de Richemont was nearby. Although he held the title of Constable of

France, Richemont had been banned from the court by the dauphin after a quarrel with La Trémoïlle. His help, therefore, was not entirely welcome. Alençon, in fact, told Joan that if Richemont joined them, he would leave.

Joan calmed him down, telling him that they needed Richemont and his thousand soldiers. Word had just been received that Talbot, Fastolf, and an English army would arrive at any time. The combined French forces attacked Beaugency, which, not knowing of the approaching English army, accepted surrender terms. On the morning of June 17, the English marched away, having taken an oath not to fight again for at least ten days.

Talbot and Fastolf had no idea that the city had fallen. They marched south, confident of trapping the French between themselves and the Beaugency garrison. When they arrived, they found the French drawn up in battle formation on a hill above them. The English sent messengers to challenge the French to a battle. Joan replied, "Go and camp for today, because it is quite late. But tomorrow, at the pleasure of God and Our Lady, we will look more closely at you."[8] Talbot and Fastolf then retreated toward Meung. They were unable to dislodge the French from the fortified bridge, but did manage to free their countrymen from inside the castle.

The next day, Saturday, June 18, Alençon was unsure what to do. He asked Joan, who said, "Have all of you good spurs?" Asked if she meant that they would be retreating, she said that, no, the English would be beaten "and you must have good spurs to pursue them."[9]

The Battle of Patay

The English began taking up a position among rows of hedges near the village of Patay. Talbot was sure the French would come that way looking for them. The French did come, but could not find the English in the thickly wooded area. As the French scouts searched, they startled a deer, which bounded away—as fortune would have it—directly into the English position. The English, thinking the French were upon them, raised a shout. The French, thus alerted to the enemy's position, attacked.

The English were not yet ready and were overwhelmed. More than two thousand were killed while the French lost only a handful. Fastolf escaped, but Talbot, England's great general, was taken prisoner along with many other top officers.

The war might have ended much sooner if the French had followed the Battle of Patay by marching on Paris. The English were defeated and disorganized. The citizens of Paris had no great love for their foreign masters and might well have helped Joan's army expel them. Philip of Burgundy, his English allies on the run and Charles in control of Paris, might have come to terms.

On to Reims

Joan was determined, however, to go to Reims. Her voices had made it clear to her that the coronation must come first. She insisted to the dauphin that they must begin the journey without delay. Charles, as reluctant as Joan was eager, told her that perhaps she ought to rest a few days. Joan burst into tears and withdrew from the castle, spending two days and nights in a nearby field. It was not until June 29 that the army, without Richemont, whom the dauphin would not pardon, departed for Reims. Charles rode at its head. Beside him was Joan, carrying her banner.

The cities along their route were loyal to the duke of Burgundy. The first, Auxerre, surrendered without a fight. Next came Troyes, the city where the treaty disinheriting the dauphin had been signed nine years earlier. Joan had sent a letter to the people there, urging them to open their gates to the dauphin in order to avoid bloodshed. Instead, the city leaders threw the letter on a fire and, when the French army approached, sent out a small body of soldiers as a show of force. After a brief skirmish, the soldiers retreated into Troyes.

For two days, messengers went back and forth. When the city leaders refused to surrender, Charles held a council. Should they attack the city or simply pass it by? Joan said, "Order your people to come and besiege the town of Troyes, and lose no more time in such long councils. In God's Name, before three days are gone, I will bring you into this town by favor or force."[10]

Joan began directing preparations for a siege. Cannons were moved into firing range. The ditch around the city wall was filled with sticks so that it could be crossed. Seeing all this, the leaders of Troyes lost their nerve and agreed to a surrender. Charles rode into the city on July 9, Joan again at his side.

Entry Into Reims

As the end of the journey neared, Charles, fearful to the last, was afraid Reims might offer some resistance. Joan assured him that it would not, and the city leaders, indeed, came out to surrender to him when the army approached. Some of the leading Burgundians had already left the city. Among them was Pierre Cauchon, bishop of Beauvais, who in a few months would preside at her trial.

Charles entered Reims on Saturday, July 16. A large crowd gathered, curious to see not only the dauphin and the famous Pucelle, but also Regnault of Chartres, who had been their archbishop for years but who, since the city was Burgundian, had never been there. Now, for once, Charles wasted no time. The coronation was set for the next day. Workers spent the night making preparations.

The Coronation

Charles entered the great cathedral at nine o'clock the next morning. Of the twelve great nobles of France—six

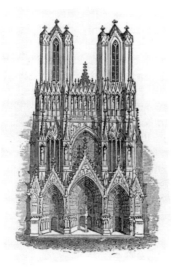

The coronation of Charles took place in the cathedral at Reims on July 16, 1429. Most French kings were crowned in the cathedral, which was built from the 1200s to 1430. Though it was damaged in World War I (1914–1918), it was repaired in 1937 and is called the Cathedral of Notre Dame today.

lords and six churchmen—who by tradition should have all been there, only three attended. One of the three, Regnault, was to perform the ceremony. All of those who did not attend were either enemies, such as Philip of Burgundy, or were fearful of getting on the bad side of the English.

Joan's rightful place would have been back among other army officers. Instead, a witness reported, "the Maid was always at the king's side, holding his standard in her hand."[11] It was a sight sure to arouse jealousy in some of the great lords of France, particularly La Trémoïlle.

The ceremony ended, and the dauphin was now officially King Charles VII. After the twelve nobles, or their substitutes, had made formal homage, it was Joan's turn. As she had many times in the past, she embraced him around the knees and said, "Gentle King, now has God's pleasure been accomplished."[12]

Joan's mission was also accomplished. She had left Domrémy only six short months before. It must have been a proud moment for her, and yet a sad one, as well. She suspected, or perhaps the voices had told her, that the coronation was the peak of her career. Triumphs were in the past; tragedy was in the future.

Paris and Compiègne

Joan of Arc's rise had been spectacular and swift. Her unshakeable faith in her mission had given those around her—even the reluctant King Charles VII—a sense of purpose and urgency. As the magic of those early months went away, however, so did the confidence France had in Joan.

At the time of the coronation in Reims, however, she was hailed as the savior of France. In the coming months, she would be asked to touch rosary beads and other items in order to bless them. Laughing, she said, "Touch them yourselves. Your touch will do them as much good as mine."[1] Still, people regarded her as a living saint.

Joan's popularity and her growing reputation were major factors in her downfall. They aroused jealousy and envy not only in the king's advisers, but also in the king. Like many small-minded persons, Charles detested greatness in others. A contemporary chronicler, Georges Chastellain, wrote that

> it was his habit ... when one had been raised high in his company even to the summit of the wheel, that then he began to be annoyed with him, and at the first occasion that could provide some sort of justification, he willfully reversed that person from high to low.[2]

Truce With Burgundy

Reims was the top of Joan's wheel, the peak of her influence. Immediately after the coronation, she urged the king to seize the moment and march on Paris. Charles's style, however, was compromise, not confrontation. More was going on behind the scenes than Joan realized. Philip of Burgundy had sent representatives to Reims to negotiate with the king or, more likely, with La Trémoïlle. The result was a truce of fifteen days, after which Philip was to surrender Paris to the king. In fact, Philip was playing for time, knowing that a new English army had landed in Normandy and was on the way to Paris.

By the time the truce was agreed to in early August, much to Joan's disgust, Charles was heading not to Paris, but back to the safety of the Loire. He intended to cross the Seine River at Bray, but the English held the bridge, and the French were forced to turn back north.

The duke of Bedford, meanwhile, had reinforced his army and had moved south along the Seine. The two armies came near one another at Montépilloy. Bedford sent an insulting letter of challenge to "you ... who at present without cause call yourself king" and are accompanied by "a woman of a disorderly and infamous life and dissolute [lacking restraint] manners dressed in the clothes of a man."[3] On August 15, the two sides faced one another in battle formation, yet neither side moved to attack. Finally, the English rode off for Paris, and Charles continued north. More towns surrendered to him peacefully, including Compiègne about fifty miles north of Paris, which later was to play an important part in Joan's life.

Another Truce

By now, the fifteen-day truce had expired, and there was no sign of Paris's surrendering. On August 21, 1429, however, another Burgundian envoy reached the king. A week later, a new truce, this one for four months, was signed. This agreement contained the curious clause that gave Duke Philip the right to defend Paris against attack, even from the king's army.

Joan, meanwhile, was already at Paris. She had been disappointed that no battle took place at Montépilloy and was growing bored as the king dallied at Compiègne, northeast of the capital. She told Alençon, "My fair duke, equip your men and those of the other captains. By my Martin [baton], I want to go to see Paris from closer than I have ever seen it."[4] The faithful Alençon obeyed, and—even though La Trémoïlle objected—a strong force headed south on

76

August 23, arriving at Saint Denis, just north of Paris, three days later.

Joan expected the king to join the army, but a week went by without any sign of him. Alençon found him about twenty miles to the south at Senlis and extracted from him a promise to come to Paris. Charles at last arrived at Saint Denis on September 7. An attack had been planned for days, but Joan was waiting on the king to give his permission, which he reluctantly did, even though he had signed the truce with Burgundy a few days before. The attack would take place the next day, even though it was a religious holiday celebrating the birth of Mary, mother of Jesus of Nazareth. Joan's voices had told her not to fight on that day, but for once she ignored them. She said at her trial that it was because others insisted. It may also have been due to her own impatience.

Attack on Paris

Nevertheless, the attack on Paris began at about two o'clock the next afternoon. Two ditches surrounded the walls of Paris. The outer ditch was dry, the inner filled with water. Under Joan's direction, the soldiers brought bundles of sticks and brush, filling the outer ditch so that they could cross over. They tried to do the same at the inner ditch, but the water was too deep, and the bundles floated away as soon as they were thrown in.

Joan crossed the outer ditch and used a lance to probe the water in the other ditch to test the depth. As

Source Document

The Maid took her standard in her hand and with the first troops entered the ditches toward the swine market. The assault was long and hard, and it was wondrous to hear the noise and the explosion of the cannons and the culverins [smaller guns] that those inside the city fired against those outside, and all manner of blows in such great abundance that they were beyond being counted. The assault lasted from about the hour of midday until about the hour of nightfall. After the sun had set, the Maid was hit by a crossbow bolt [arrow] in her thigh. After she had been hit, she insisted even more strenuously that everyone should approach the walls so that the place would be taken; but because it was night and she was wounded and the men-at-arms were weary from the day-long assault, the lord of Gaucourt and others came to the Maid and against her will carried [her] out of the ditch, and so the assault ended.[5]

Percival de Cagny, chronicler of the duke of Alençon, wrote this account of Joan's wound during the unsuccessful assault on Paris.

she did so, she was struck in the thigh by an arrow. At the same time, a soldier nearby holding her banner was hit in the heel. When he raised the visor of his helmet so he could see to pull out the arrow, another struck him between the eyes. He fell dead, and Joan's banner fell to the ground—an unlucky sign.

Against her will, Joan was carried away from the walls to safety. The attack continued throughout the afternoon, but without success. As darkness fell, the French retreated to Saint Denis.

A Change of Heart

The next day, Joan and Alençon were preparing to launch another assault when they received word to return immediately to Saint Denis by order of the king. There, to Joan's dismay, they discovered Charles had ordered that no more attacks were to occur until a council met to decide whether or not to continue.

Meanwhile, Philip of Burgundy sent more envoys with more promises that Paris would eventually be surrendered. La Trémoïlle, whose goal was a negotiated peace between the king and the duke, with himself to be chief minister of a united France, counseled Charles to withdraw. It would be only days, a few months at the most, before Paris was his, the king was told. Charles agreed, and the army returned to Senlis.

Once in Senlis, Joan pleaded with the king for more military action. Charles would not listen. The legend of invincibility was gone, and with it the king's confidence in her. If God had once guided her, Charles thought, he had now abandoned her. Instead, Charles listened to the counsel of La Trémoïlle and others whose advice was much more to his liking.

Alençon Departs

Joan was not the only one unhappy with the idleness of court life. Alençon left for Normandy to try to recapture some of his lands there. Joan begged to go with him, but Regnault and La Trémoïlle would not permit it. Joan would never see her closest friend again.

Weeks dragged by. Finally, it was La Trémoïlle who found a use for Joan. He ordered her to capture two small towns on the Loire, Saint Pierre le Moûtier and La Charité.

Joan set out with a small army in late October. Saint Pierre fell on November 4, but La Charité proved much more difficult. Most of the army's supplies had been used up at Saint Pierre. Joan wrote to King Charles, asking for food and equipment. She received nothing, and the siege had to be lifted. It was another defeat, and the rumors that Joan had lost her power grew.

Joan spent most of the winter at Sully, in a castle belonging to La Trémoïlle. It was not until early March that she rejoined the king. Charles was still confident that negotiations with Burgundy would succeed, even though Philip was becoming increasingly aggressive. The citizens of Reims felt threatened and wrote a letter to Joan asking for help. She replied on March 16, 1430, urging them to stand fast and promising that she would lift any siege.

Compiègne

The citizens of Compiègne also felt very insecure. They had proclaimed their loyalty to the king the previous July, but now Charles, as a gesture of good will to Burgundy, offered to give the city back. The citizens refused, and the city's commander, Guillaume de Flavy, began to prepare for an eventual attack.

In late April 1430, Joan decided to take matters into her own hands. Without the king's knowledge, she set out for Compiègne, perhaps hoping Charles would eventually follow her, as he had to Paris. He did not, and the two would never meet again.

Joan stopped in Lagny. While she was there, she was asked to revive an infant who apparently had died unbaptized. She said she had no such power, but that she would pray for its soul. As she did so, the baby revived long enough to be baptized before it died. This would be one source of the charges of witchcraft made against her.

From Lagny, she moved on to Melun. While there, she said later, she was visited by Saint Catherine and Saint Margaret. Her voices long had told her she had only a short time. This time they were more specific, saying, "You wilt be taken before Saint John's Day [June 24] and so it must be: do not torment thyself about it: be resigned; God will help thee."[6]

The Burgundian Threat

In early May, King Charles finally realized that Philip of Burgundy had no intention of keeping his word and, indeed, was threatening to recapture everything north of the Loire. Charles had few resources but realized that one of them was Joan of Arc. He ordered her to go to Compiègne and sent reinforcements, including Bishop Regnault and the count of Vendôme.

Meanwhile, the Burgundians were drawing closer. On May 16, the town of Choisy surrendered, and its defenders were allowed to retreat to Compiègne. A few days later, they captured the town of Margny, which lay just across the Oise River from Compiègne.

On May 23, Joan, Vendôme, and Flavy decided to launch a surprise attack on Margny. Wearing rich cloth-of-gold over her armor and carrying her banner, Joan led the way across the drawbridge over the Oise. Boats had been placed on the far bank in case the soldiers had to retreat swiftly into the city.

The attack was a failure. John of Luxembourg, a vassal of Burgundy, happened to be in Margny and, on seeing the French, sent a rider to bring reinforcements. They came quickly, and the French were soon outnumbered. Joan tried to rally them, but the respect she had commanded at Orléans and elsewhere had vanished. The French fell back toward Compiègne, scrambling into the boats and across the bridge.

Capture

Joan, with a few companions, remained on the far side of the bridge, fighting to give the rest of their forces more time to cross. Guillaume de Flavy then ordered

During a fierce battle at the bridge leading to Compiègne, Joan was captured by the English.

the drawbridge raised. Joan was trapped outside the walls.

Historians have debated ever since whether Flavy deliberately shut Joan out of Compiègne. After all, he was a nephew of Regnault of Chartres and a direct subordinate of La Trémoïlle, no friends of Joan's. Also, the drawbridge protected an outer gate, not the main gate into the city. Whether Flavy's action was spurred by treachery or panic, no one will ever know.

Either way, it spelled doom for Joan. Her little band was surrounded. A Burgundian archer grabbed her rich cloak and pulled her from her horse. Soldiers crowded around her, each demanding that she surrender to him. "I have already made submission and plighted my faith to another [God]," she said, "and to Him will I keep my word."[7] At last an officer, Lionel of Wandomme, appeared, and Joan—who, despite her brave words, had no choice—formally surrendered to him.

Joan's military career had lasted a year. Only one more year remained to her. It would be filled, not with the excitement of battle, but with the darkness and despair of prison and, at the end, with death.

Rouen

After Joan of Arc's capture outside the walls of Compiègne, she was in the hands of two sets of enemies. The first, the intellectuals of the University of Paris, demanded her dishonor and disgrace. The second, the English, wanted nothing less than her death.

The University of Paris wanted a unified Church ruled by a council in which it would be the dominant force, along with a pope. Such a plan needed a strong political base, and university leaders saw one in a joint Anglo-French monarchy. Joan had upset their plans by reviving hopes for an independent France.

Furthermore, the plan would demand absolute obedience to Church leaders. Joan was a threat because she claimed her authority came directly from God. To establish its own authority, the university had to discredit Joan, not only in the eyes of the French, but also before the rest of Europe.

English Motives

The motives of the English were more straightforward. They needed to show both their own soldiers and the French that Joan's power came not from God, but from Satan. The English had dominated most of the Hundred Years' War. It was not enough, however, to prove Joan a witch. She had to die. The simple reason was that the English were afraid of her. A Burgundian chronicler wrote that the English "feared no other captain or commander as much as they had always feared, until this day [of her capture], that Pucelle."[1]

Some of her supposed allies were not at all unhappy to see her a prisoner. Regnault of Chartres wrote that Joan had deserved to be captured "because she would not take advice, but would follow her own will," and La Trémoïlle was said to be "overcome with delight."[2]

And what about King Charles, the person whom she had so greatly aided and in whose service she had been made prisoner? He said nothing and did nothing. He made no attempt to rescue Joan because of the military situation. He also never tried to ransom her, the usual salvation of important prisoners. Charles VII would go on to become a strong and effective ruler, but a biographer of Joan, Vita Sackville-West, believes his abandonment of Joan of Arc left "a residue of contemptible treachery which must for ever be associated with his name."[3]

Joan the Prisoner

Meanwhile, Joan's captivity was not too harsh, at least initially. Lionel of Wandomme had yielded her to his overlord, John of Luxembourg. She was first housed in Beaulieu Castle but, after an attempted escape, was moved to John's castle at Beaurevoir.

Although physically comfortable, Joan, like any other prisoner, was anxious about her fate. Only a few days after her capture, the University of Paris had written to John asking him to surrender her "since she is strongly suspected of various crimes smacking of heresy."[4]

John hesitated, and the university leaders reconsidered. If John would not yield Joan to them on religious principles, perhaps he would sell her. They approached the duke of Bedford, uncle and regent in France for the boy king Henry VI. A deal was made. Bedford would supply the money to pay John of Luxembourg, and Joan would be brought to trial by the Church on charges of heresy and witchcraft.

It was a perfect solution for Bedford. Joan would not be tried by Englishmen, but by her French countrymen. The trial would be conducted by the Church, not the military, which was important because it would have been difficult to execute her as a legitimate prisoner of war. Furthermore, Bedford had the perfect man to place in charge of the trial—Pierre Cauchon, bishop of Beauvais.

Cauchon

Cauchon was a dedicated supporter of the plan for having two kings. He had grown rich as an agent for English interests and had been made bishop of Beauvais in 1420. His reasons for persecuting Joan of Arc, however, were personal as well as political. He had been forced to flee from Reims to Beauvais just before the king's coronation. The next month, the people of Beauvais declared their loyalty for the king and expelled Cauchon, giving him good cause to hate Joan.

Joan somehow learned of what was being planned for her. Although she would later say that her voices had told her to be patient, she grew so desperate that she attempted to escape by leaping off the top of the castle tower. Despite the fall of about seventy feet, she was not seriously hurt.

By November 1430, the negotiations were complete, and Joan was handed over to the English. The next month, John of Luxembourg received ten thousand francs, a small amount of which went to Lionel of Wandomme, her original captor. A site for the trial still had not been determined. Bedford demanded the trial be held in the heavily English city of Rouen in Normandy.

A trial in Rouen posed some technical difficulties. Luckily for Bedford, Joan had been captured within the area around Beauvais that Cauchon had been bishop for, meaning that Cauchon could conduct the trial. By law, however, the trial had to take place in

Beauvais, and Beauvais was still loyal to Charles. Bedford got around the law by forcing the Church leaders in Rouen to grant Cauchon special permission to act as a judge in a city where he had no legal authority.

Rouen

Any gentle treatment of Joan ended abruptly at Rouen, where she was taken on December 23. Since hers was to be a Church trial, she should have been kept in a Church prison, tended by nuns. Instead, she was shut up in a dark cell on the second floor of a tower, with her legs chained to a large block of wood. Her guards were five English soldiers, apparently selected for their brutality. They constantly made fun of their captive. They tried to physically molest her, but were stopped by order of the duchess of Bedford, sister to the duke of Burgundy.

Cauchon had sent agents to Domrémy, hoping to find something in Joan's past to use against her. His search was a failure. One investigator reported he found "nothing about Joan that he would not wish to find about his own sister."[5] Therefore, Cauchon hoped to get her to confess, either by force or by trickery. The harsh treatment was intended to break Joan's spirit.

The Condemnation Trial Begins

What became known as Joan's Condemnation Trial began on January 9, 1431, three days after Joan's nineteenth birthday. Cauchon and the other judges spent more than six weeks before the trial digging for information, seeking witnesses, and trying to come up with evidence against their prisoner. They found nothing and decided that Joan must be convicted on her own words.

She first appeared before the court on February 21. She was not allowed a defending counsel and stood alone, facing forty-four Church leaders, doctors of theology, and doctors of law. They soon found out that Joan's spirit was unbroken. Asked to swear an oath to tell the truth, she replied, "I know not upon what you wish to question me; perhaps you may ask me of things which I ought not to tell you."[6] She stood firm against all arguments, finally agreeing to swear to answer only the questions she thought proper. Some things about her saints and what they had told her, for instance, she would not reveal "even if it cost me my head."[7]

The judges asked her about her childhood. They accused her of having carried a mandrake, a magic charm. She denied it and said she had never even seen one. They asked her about her sword and banner, hinting that she had enchanted them. They accused her of trying to perform miracles, such as reviving the baby at Lagny. They accused her of attempting the sin of suicide by leaping from the tower at Beaurevoir. She insisted she had been trying to escape.

Again and again, they asked her why she wore men's clothes, as she still did during the trial. "I did not take it by the advice of any man in the world," she answered, not mentioning Jean de Metz. "I did not

One of the biggest issues during Joan's trial was the fact that she wore men's clothes. This was uncommon in the fifteenth century, and Joan's accusers felt it was a sign that she was a witch.

take this dress or do anything but by the command of Our Lord and of the Angels."[8]

Joan's Conduct

Joan confounded every attempt to trick her. Asked if her voices had told her if she would be set free, she said that was no part of the case against her. When the judges tried to get her to contradict herself by returning to various subjects after several days, she would simply say that she had already answered those questions, and ask that they go to the next question.

Even when faced with complex religious questions that would have stumped even her judges, Joan always had a well-thought-out answer. She was asked, for instance, if she were in the grace of God, something Christians are supposed to strive for but not to know for certain. If she answered yes, she would presume to know God's will. If she answered no, she would seem to deny that her voices came from God. She said, "If I am not, may God place me there; if I am, may God so keep me."[9] Jean Massieu, one of the scribes who recorded the trial, later said admiringly, "No man of letters [highly educated] could have replied better."[10]

Cauchon realized that he was getting nowhere. Indeed, Joan seemed to be winning some friends among the judges. He decided to abandon the public hearings. In the future, all questioning would be done in Joan's cell by a small and carefully selected group.

The Questions Continue

The questions and the answers were much the same. As the days wore on, the judges concentrated on an old subject, Joan's wearing of men's clothes, and on a new one, her possible lack of obedience to the Church. The second point was crucial to the scholars of the University of Paris. In their eyes, social order depended on absolute obedience to the Church and its popes, cardinals, and bishops. Joan obeyed what she termed "a higher authority"—not the earthly Church, but God, saints, and angels. Repeatedly, Joan was asked if she would submit to the Church. "My words and deeds are all in God's Hands: in all, I wait upon him," she answered.[11]

Joan's forthright and eloquent answers soon forced Cauchon to abandon any pretense that the trial was fair. He ordered judges who protested that questions were unfair to be quiet. One judge, Jean de Chatillon, complained so much that he was dismissed by Cauchon. Guillaume Manchon, a scribe, later said Cauchon ordered some of Joan's testimony to be changed and other parts to be left out of the record entirely.

Seventy Charges

The private questioning ended on March 18, 1431, and the second part of the trial, called the "Ordinary," began March 27. Seventy articles, or charges, were read to Joan covering everything from wearing men's clothes to saying that her voices spoke French instead of English. She denied everything and was returned to

93

her cell. Cauchon and the judges must have realized that many of the charges were not only unfounded, but also ridiculous. They spent the first week in April reducing the seventy articles to twelve.

On April 18 in her cell and again on May 2 in public, Joan was forced to listen to sermons warning her of her danger and urging her to admit her guilt and be forgiven by the Church. She refused. On May 9, the warnings took on a darker tone. She was taken to a chamber and shown various instruments of torture. "Truly," she said, "if you were to tear me limb from limb, and separate soul from body, I will tell you nothing more: and, if I were to say anything else, I should always afterwards declare that you made me say it by force."[12] Cauchon decided nothing would be gained by torture, and Joan was returned to her cell.

The Abjuration

On May 24, 1431, almost exactly a year after she was captured, Joan was taken to a large cemetery in which there were two platforms. Joan was placed on one, along with one of her judges—a priest named Guillaume Erard—and Jean Massieu. On the other were Cauchon and several dignitaries, including the earl of Warwick and the bishop of Winchester from England.

Erard preached a lengthy sermon on obedience to the Church. At the end, he reviewed the charges against Joan and called on her to abjure, or to take back her testimony and admit guilt. Joan did not understand the word. Erard told Massieu to explain it to her, which he did, then saying that if she did not abjure, she would be burned at the stake.

Cauchon rose and began to read the sentence of the court. Joan was to be excommunicated, or cut off, from the Church and handed over to the civil authorities to be burned. (The Church itself could not carry out executions.) Massieu and Erard continued to urge her to sign a piece of paper, called an abjuration, that had been thrust into her hand. Joan protested that she could not read. Erard said, "You shall abjure at once, or you shall be burned."[13]

Joan could see the executioner and his cart waiting outside the cemetery. She could hear the death sentence and the pleas for her to sign the abjuration. Her willpower gave way, and she made her mark on the paper. Witnesses later said that the paper contained no more than seven or eight lines of writing. The document later entered into the record had been greatly expanded, containing more than fifty lines.

English Anger

Despite Joan's plea to be taken to a Church court, Cauchon ordered her returned to the same cell. As she was led away, a commotion broke out among the judges. The English were furious. They had expected to see Joan executed. One of the English priests told Cauchon he was being too easy on Joan. "You lie!" the bishop replied. "It is my duty, on account of my profession, to seek the salvation of the soul and body of this Jeanne."[14]

Perhaps this was true. Perhaps Cauchon, impressed with Joan, had no wish to see her die. Her abjuration, her renouncing of her voices, served his purpose. And yet, the abjuration may all have been part of his scheme. One witness said that when the earl of Warwick protested that the English had wasted their money buying Joan, Cauchon said, "Take no heed to it, my lord; we shall soon have her again."[15]

Joan Condemned

Back in her cell, Joan's head was shaved as a sign of repentance, or regret for sins. She was given a woman's dress to put on. A bag containing the men's clothes, however, was left in the cell. Four days later, Cauchon heard that Joan had begun wearing male clothes again. He confronted her. She told him, "I have damned myself to save my life! . . . my Voices have said to me since Thursday: 'You have done a great evil in declaring that what you have done was wrong.' All I said and revoked, I said for fear of the fire."[16]

At this, the scribe taking down her words wrote two of his own—"*responsio mortifera,*" or fatal answer. When Cauchon left the cell, he said to the earl of Warwick: "Be of good cheer. It is done."[17]

On the next day, May 29, the judges met and unanimously condemned Joan as a relapsed heretic. For this there was only one sentence, death by burning. Early on May 30, 1431, Cauchon sent a priest, Martin Ladvenu, to Joan's cell to tell her what awaited her and to hear her confession. Joan cried out, "Alas! am

Source Document

On one occasion . . . when I counseled her to submit to the Council of Bâle, Jeanne asked what a General Council was. I answered her, that it was an assembly of the whole Church Universal and of Christendom, and that in this Council there were some of her side as well [as] of the English side. Having heard and understood this, she began to cry: "Oh! if in that place there are any of our side, I am quite willing to give myself up and to submit to the Council of Bâle." And immediately, in great rage and indignation, the Bishop of Beauvais began to call out: "Hold your tongue, in the devil's name!" and told the Notary he was to be careful to make no note of the submission she had made to the General Council of Bâle. On account of these things . . . the English and their officers threatened me terribly, so that, had I not kept silence, they would have thrown me into the Seine [River].[18]

At her Condemnation Trial, Joan's judges were determined to deny her any chance at appeal, according to this testimony from Isambart de La Pierre at her Nullification Trial.

I to be so horribly and cruelly treated? Alas! that my body, whole and entire, which has never been corrupted, should today be consumed and burned to ashes! Ah! I would far rather have my head cut off, seven times over, than be thus burned!"[19]

Cauchon entered the cell. At once Joan said, "Bishop, I die through you . . . for this I summon you before God [to answer to God for her death]."[20] Cauchon argued that she had condemned herself.

Last Communion

Cauchon left Joan's cell. Soon, he received a request. Joan wanted to receive communion, a holy ceremony of the Church. Since Joan had been excommunicated, this should not have been allowed. Cauchon, however, agreed. For the communion, special bread and wine were given to Joan by Ladvenu.

Finally, it was time. Joan was dressed in women's clothing and led to a waiting cart. Her last visitor had been a priest named Pierre Maurice. She asked him where she would be that night. Maurice asked if she still trusted in God. She replied that she did and, God willing, she would soon be in heaven.

In a few hours, it was all over. Joan's ashes were thrown into the Seine River. All that remained were her heart and some internal organs. The executioner, according to Father Isambart's testimony, said he had tried to burn them but could not.

Joan's spirit lived on in the French people, who were still battling for their country.

Chapter 9

The Triumph of France

Joan of Arc's life had ended, but the Hundred Years' War dragged on. She had, however, given the French two new psychological weapons. First, they realized once again that the English, considered invincible since the battle at Agincourt, could be beaten. Second, they had a rallying point, however reluctant, in King Charles VII. It would take another twenty-two years, but Joan's dream of a united France would come true.

The duke of Bedford was well aware of the symbolic significance of Charles's coronation. He tried to counter it by having one of his own. He brought nine-year-old Henry VI over from England to be crowned Henri II of France in Paris. The ceremony, on December 16, 1431, was largely ignored by the French, and the banquet afterward turned into a riot.

The English were unsuccessful on the battlefield, as well. The city of Chartres was lost in 1432, and

Bedford permanently damaged his health during an unsuccessful assault on Lagny.

Perhaps the most damaging blow to English hopes, however, was the death in November 1432 of Bedford's wife, Anne of Burgundy. Without her influence, the alliance between England and Burgundy began to weaken. In 1435, the French, Burgundians, and English met in Arras to negotiate a settlement. Bedford was too ill to attend. His place was taken by Henry Beaufort, bishop of Winchester, who had been at Joan's execution. Beaufort refused to make any concessions, and the talks ended after six weeks.

The Treaty of Arras

A week later, Bedford died. Soon afterward, the talks began once more, but this time without the English. On September 20, Philip of Burgundy and Charles VII ended their long feud and signed the Treaty of Arras. One of the key negotiators was Joan's old enemy, Georges de La Trémoïlle, who at last saw his political policy succeed.

Now, the English stood alone against the French. Philip of Burgundy would not play a major role. He was also duke of Flanders, which depended heavily on English wool. But, while he could not fight the English, at least he did not fight alongside them against the French.

Philip of Burgundy (pictured) signed the Treaty of Arras with Charles VII on September 20, 1435, ensuring that the Burgundians would no longer fight alongside the English against the French.

The English Leave Paris

Meanwhile, the people of Paris had grown weary of English occupation. In 1436, Arthur de Richemont, back in the king's good graces, besieged the city. On April 13, the Parisians opened their gates to the invaders, and the English had to flee to a fortress. After some negotiations, they were forced to leave. "No one was ever jeered and booed as they were," a witness wrote.[1]

In England, meanwhile, those closest to King Henry VI wanted peace with France. Led by the earl of Suffolk, they arranged a truce by which Henry would marry Margaret of Anjou, King Charles's niece, and the French county of Le Maine would be surrendered by England. The marriage took place in 1445. The new queen of England quickly gained control of her husband, who had inherited the feeblemindedness of his grandfather on his mother's side, Charles VI of France. She did everything she could to bring peace on terms favorable to the French.

A Different Charles

Charles VII took advantage of the new mood in England. This was not the hesitant, indecisive dauphin Joan had fought for. Charles had matured. He was determined to rid his country of the English. His experiences in his court had made him a shrewd and ruthless politician.

Charles was no soldier, but he knew the value of a strong military. He reorganized the French army and made it the first permanent army in Europe, paid in peacetime as well as during war. While his ancestors had gloried in hand-to-hand combat, Charles appreciated the less honorable but much more effective results of gunfire. He spent large sums of money on the development of artillery by Jean Bureau, whose cannons played a major role in the expulsion of the English from the area around Paris.

Charles's new target was Normandy, which had been English since it was conquered by Henry V in 1417. On October 16, 1449, the French army assaulted the capital, Rouen, where Joan had died eighteen years earlier. They were repelled by the English led by Talbot, but then settled down to besiege the city.

The Fall of Rouen

The people of Rouen remembered all too well the suffering they had endured during the siege by the English in 1417. They had no wish to go through another siege, especially against fellow Frenchmen.

They rioted against the English and opened the city gates to the French. The English were eventually allowed to leave the city, but only after surrendering Talbot as a hostage.

The fall of Rouen alarmed England. Those opposed to Queen Margaret's policy of peace were led by Richard, duke of York. They managed to get an army sent to try to recover what had been lost. It was, however, a modest force of only four thousand men under Thomas Kyriell. They landed at Cherbourg in March 1450 and marched toward Bayeux, which was being besieged by the French. Kyriell, however, never reached Bayeux. Instead, he was met near the village of Fromingy on April 15 by a French army.

The English took up a defensive position, just as they had done at Crécy, Poitiers, and Agincourt, trying to get the French to charge. Instead, the French brought up cannons and, under an artillery barrage, it was the English who were forced to charge. They were routed, and Kyriell was made a prisoner.

After the Battle of Fromingy, it was only a matter of time before Normandy was conquered. Caen surrendered in June, and Falaise the next month, part of the bargain being the release of Talbot. Finally, only the port of Cherbourg remained in English hands. It was besieged and came under heavy attack from Bureau's guns. The city surrendered on August 12, and Normandy was French again after more than thirty years.

Guyenne

Earlier in his career, King Charles would have been content with the conquest of Normandy. Not now. He quickly turned to Guyenne, which was a far different situation. While the people of Normandy had barely tolerated English rule, Guyenne had been English for more than three hundred years. The people considered themselves more English than French.

It was natural, then, that they would combine with the English to stop the first French invasion in 1450. The second invasion a year later, however, was more successful. The French, commanded by Jean Dunois and helped by Bureau's artillery, captured the capital city of Guyenne, Bordeaux, on June 30, 1451. The last city, Bayonne, fell three weeks later. The French controlled Guyenne—but not for long.

The people of Guyenne hated their new masters. In 1452, they sent a delegation to London, promising to help if England would send an army. York's war party was in control of Parliament at the time, and a sizeable force under Talbot sailed in October.

The French had expected Talbot to land in Normandy, as had so many other invaders over the last century. The old warrior surprised them, however, sailing straight to Guyenne. The people did what they had promised, opening the gates of Bordeaux to the English on October 21. By the new year, all of western Guyenne was English once more.

The Battle of Castillon

Charles was determined to take Guyenne back. In the spring of 1453, he launched an attack from three directions, all heading toward Bordeaux. Talbot knew that his only chance was to take on these invaders one at a time. His first move was in July against the French army besieging the town of Castillon.

The siege featured something new in warfare, a fortified artillery park. Bureau had built trenches leading toward the town. Cannons were hauled through them and set up behind an earthen wall strengthened with tree trunks. From this position of relative safety, the French could pound the walls of the town.

Talbot arrived on July 17 at the head of thirteen hundred mounted men. While he was waiting for the rest of his army to catch up, a messenger arrived from the town. He told Talbot the French were retreating. Talbot did not want the French to escape and decided to attack the fortification.

The French, in fact, were not retreating. What the townspeople had seen was only the dust raised by a few horses. Therefore, as Talbot charged the fortification, Bureau's guns opened fire, mowing down the English riders.

The English charge stalled and then fell back. At that point, a force of about a thousand mounted Frenchmen attacked from one side. Talbot tried to rally his troops, but was pinned to the ground by his horse when it was killed by a gunshot. As the great

Source Document

But at last when the said English and Gascons [people of Guyenne] saw themselves oppressed and overwhelmed, and were running short of food, they were very amazed for they saw all the strong places and fortresses of the surrounding countryside reduced by force of arms, and put in full and entire obedience to the King of France. They asked for favourable terms. The king agreed to this for two reasons; first, he was ready to render good for evil; secondly, he took account of the great mortality [death rate] in his camp so that in order to get a change of air, he was ready to make an agreement with the English in the following form. . . . The town and city of Bordeaux was to be restored and given up to the King of France, and all the inhabitants would remain his true and obedient subjects, and would take an oath never to rebel again or rise against the crown of France, and to recognize and affirm that the King of France was their sovereign lord. Then the English had permission to leave by means of their ships either for England or Calais, as should seem best to them.[2]

The end of the Hundred Years' War came with the surrender of Bordeaux on October 17, 1453. This contemporary description was written by Jean Chartier.

English commander lay helpless, a French soldier killed him with an axe.

End of the War

The Battle of Castillon doomed the English cause. Bordeaux surrendered to the French on October 19, 1453. The few English survivors sailed away, never to return. Neither side knew it at the time, but the Hundred Years' War was over.

While the war was over, the story of Joan of Arc was not. Charles was aware that his abandonment of Joan was a mark against him. In addition, her conviction of heresy—the suggestion that she had not been divinely inspired—cast doubt on his own character, since he had believed in her. When he entered Rouen as king in 1450, he gained access to the records of the trial conducted almost twenty years earlier. He ordered an investigation into the circumstances of the trial and execution. Three years later, Joan would be put on trial again. This time the verdict would be far different.

Chapter 10

Redemption and Legacy

Twenty-five years after her death, Joan of Arc was placed on trial once more. This time the goal was to clear her name rather than to tarnish it. She would be found innocent of all charges against her, but it would be almost another five hundred years before she would receive sainthood for her deeds. Historians still debate whether or not she had any real impact on the Hundred Years' War.

After King Charles VII ordered an investigation of Joan's trial in 1450, a summary drawn up by legal scholars said the verdict should be overturned. Only the pope, however, could order a new trial. The summary was presented to Pope Nicolas V in 1452, but he took no action, not wanting to widen the split between England and France.

Finally, the war was over, and there was a new pope, Calixtus III. After studying the summary, he authorized a new trial with the formal request to be brought by Joan's family.

A Mother's Plea

Joan's father had died, but on November 7, 1455, her elderly mother entered the great Cathedral of Notre Dame at Paris. Surrounded by family members and a delegation from Orléans, she approached three bishops who had been appointed by the pope to oversee the new trial. In a sobbing voice, she told how her daughter had been subjected to "a perfidious [dishonest], violent, and iniquitous [sinful] trial" and then made to "die most cruelly by fire."[1]

The Church court called dozens of witnesses—friends from Domrémy, soldiers from Orléans, priests from Rouen. The great and small testified, from the duke of Alençon to Bertrand LaCloppe, a laborer from Domrémy. The testimony was entirely favorable to Joan and forms most of what is known about her early life. Most of her enemies—Cauchon, Regnault of Chartres—were dead. La Trémoïlle had been banished from France. A few of her minor judges at Rouen testified, now suddenly sorry—with the English defeated—for what they had taken part in. Indeed, this "Nullification Trial" may have been just as biased in Joan's favor as the earlier trial had been against her.

A New Verdict

The verdict was proclaimed on June 7, 1456. Joan was found innocent of all charges. Furthermore, the court

ordered that on the following day a ceremony would
take place in the marketplace at Rouen. According to
the trial transcripts, it would conclude with the
"placing of a handsome cross for the perpetual
memory of the Deceased and for her salvation and
that of other deceased persons."[2]

JEANNE DARC.

---

*Since her execution, Joan of Arc has been found innocent of all
the charges brought against her and has been honored for
centuries in art and literature. This engraving was taken from a
portrait dated 1581.*

In the centuries to come, however, Joan's "perpetual memory" would fade. Her voice had been raised against authority. She, a peasant girl, had become a leader of the people. Such ideas, thought the nobles and high-ranking church members of France, were best forgotten. It was not until after the French Revolution in 1789 and the rise of common people to power that historians revived her story, and France once more found a heroine.

Saint Joan

As knowledge about Joan and her accomplishments grew, a movement was begun in 1849 by Félix Dupanloup, bishop of Orléans, to have her designated a saint by the Roman Catholic Church. As it had so often during Joan's lifetime, politics got in the way. Joan was the national heroine of France, and France's rivals were not happy about making her a saint. It was not until May 9, 1920, that she was officially declared Saint Joan by Pope Benedict XV.

Joan's place in history has been assured, but what was her actual role? Her critics argue that she made little difference in the outcome of the Hundred Years' War. The weakened English would soon have abandoned the siege of Orléans anyway, they claim. The crowning of Charles VII was of little consequence, and he soon would have reached an agreement with Philip of Burgundy in any case.

And yet, historians cannot be sure that Orléans would not have fallen to the English. If it had, all of

France south of the Loire would have been open to the invaders, and the outcome of the war might have been very different. English success in the south might have strengthened the fragile alliance between England and Burgundy.

Joan's Impact

Even so, it is true that most of Joan's impact on the events of the time was psychological rather than military. Through the relief of Orléans and the victory at Patay, Joan had shown the French that they were capable of winning on the battlefield and that it was possible for the English to lose—something they had seldom done in almost a century of fighting. True, Bedford and the English recaptured almost all they had lost, but the French never lost the memory of victory, and it would serve them well in the decades to come.

Joan had also demonstrated to a reluctant dauphin that he had it within himself to become a king. The march to his coronation at Reims was a bold and dangerous step, and boldness was completely out of character for the young Charles VII. Perhaps Joan had awakened something in the weak prince that would flower as he became a mature ruler. In addition, Joan seems to have relieved in Charles's mind the lingering doubt as to whether he was the legitimate heir.

She had also shown Charles what it would be like to be a king. He had grown up in a royal household and had been the heir to the throne, but he had never been treated as a true ruler. Such events as the ceremony in

Reims Cathedral and the triumphant entry into Troyes doubtless gave Charles a taste of kingship, and his appetite grew.

The Unanswered Question

The basic question concerning Joan of Arc—whether the voices that spoke to her were real or not—can never be answered to everyone's satisfaction. Certainly, they were real to her. Furthermore, her voices were considered real in that superstitious age by those who believed her either a saint or a witch.

Was she merely a highly imaginative teenager, carried away into fantasy by her extreme religiousness? Was she, as some have claimed, slightly insane? Or, did God choose this peasant girl as His instrument, speaking to her through saints? No one will ever know. What is known, however, is that Joan of Arc rekindled the flickering flame of French pride. She came to the aid of a beaten country and its unmotivated ruler, helping them, through her own boundless belief in her mission, to believe in themselves.

Timeline

1337—King Edward III of England proclaims himself king of France; Hundred Years' War begins.

1340—English Navy wins Battle of Sluys.

1346—English win Battle of Crécy and capture port city of Calais.

1348—"Black Death" plague ravages Europe.

1356—English win Battle of Poitiers; King John of France taken prisoner.

1360—Treaty of Brétigny signed but renounced by France in 1363.

1364—Charles V the Wise becomes king of France and begins reconquest of areas won by English.

1377—King Edward III dies; Richard II becomes king of England.

1399—Richard II removed from throne; Henry IV becomes king of England.

1407—Duke of Orléans assassinated by agents of the duke of Burgundy.

1411—Henry IV sends troops to France at request of duke of Burgundy.

1412—*January 6*: Joan of Arc born in Domrémy.

1415—Henry V of England invades Normandy and wins Battle of Agincourt.

1418—Paris surrenders to Henry V.

1419—Duke of Burgundy assassinated by agents of Charles, dauphin of France.

1420—Treaty of Troyes disinherits dauphin, names Henry V heir to French throne.

1422—Henry V dies, leaving infant son Henry VI king of England.

1424—Joan begins to hear voices she later identifies as those of saints.

1427—*October 1*: English begin siege of Orléans.

1428—*May*: Joan first sees Robert de Baudricourt in Valcouleurs.

1429—*January*: Joan's second meeting with Baudricourt.
February 22: Joan leaves Valcouleurs for Chinon, arriving on March 6.
March 8: Joan first meets the dauphin, tells him the "king's secret."
March 11: Joan questioned at Poitiers.
April: Joan leaves Chinon for Orléans, entering city on April 29.
May 8: English lift the siege of Orléans after being defeated by the French.
June 18: French win Battle of Patay.
June 29: Joan and dauphin set out for Reims.
July 7: Dauphin crowned King Charles VI in Reims.

August 26: Joan and duke of Alençon arrive outside Paris.

September 8: Attack on Paris fails; Joan is wounded.

1430—*April*: Joan leads troops to Compiègne.

May 23: Joan captured by Burgundians at Compiègne.

July–November: Joan imprisoned at Beaurevoir.

December 23: Joan arrives at Rouen.

1431—*January 9*: Joan's trial begins.

February 21: First public session of trial.

March 10: First private session of trial in Joan's cell.

March 27: "Ordinary" part of trial begins.

May 24: Joan signs statement of abjuration.

May 28: Joan resumes wearing men's clothing in her cell.

May 30: Joan burned at the stake in Rouen marketplace.

1435—Treaty of Arras ends feud between French and Burgundians.

1436—English troops forced to leave Paris.

1449—Charles VI launches invasion of Normandy.

April 15: French win Battle of Fromingy; Normandy surrenders to French.

1450—French gain control of English province of Guyenne; Charles VI opens investigation into Joan's trial.

1452—English under Talbot invade Guyenne.

1453—*July 17*: French win Battle of Castillon; Talbot killed.
October 19: English abandon Guyenne; end of Hundred Years' War.

1455—Pope Calixtus III authorizes Nullification Trial to clear Joan's name.

1456—*June 7*: Court proclaims Joan of Arc innocent.

1920—*May 9*: Joan of Arc declared a saint by Roman Catholic Church.

Chapter Notes

Chapter 1. The Marketplace

1. Polly Schoyer Brooks, *Beyond the Myth: The Story of Joan of Arc* (New York: J. B. Lippincott, 1990), p. 146.

2. W. S. Scott, trans., *The Trial of Joan of Arc* (London: The Folio Society, 1956), p. 156.

3. Régine Pernoud and Marie Véronique Clin, *Joan of Arc: Her Story* (New York: St. Martin's Press, 1998), p. 135.

4. Brooks, p. 146.

5. Pernoud and Clin, p. 136.

6. Ibid., p. 147.

7. Vita Sackville-West, *Saint Joan of Arc* (London: The Folio Society, 1995), p. 284.

Chapter 2. The Endless War

1. Michael Packe, *King Edward III* (London: Ark Paperbacks, 1985), p. 81.

2. A.R. Meyers, ed., *English Historical Documents: 1327–1485* (New York: Oxford University Press, 1969), p. 81.

3. Philip Ziegler, *The Black Death* (New York: Harper and Row, 1969), p. 135.

Chapter 3. Domrémy

1. Vita Sackville-West, *Saint Joan of Arc* (London: The Folio Society, 1995), p. 20.

2. W. S. Scott, trans., *The Trial of Joan of Arc* (London: The Folio Society, 1956), p. 67.

3. Ibid.

4. Virginia Frohlick—Saint Joan of Arc Center, "Second Public Examination," *Saint Joan of Arc's Trial of Condemnation,* n.d., <http://www.stjoan-center.com/Trials/sec02.html> (May 30, 2002).

5. Kelly DeVries, *Joan of Arc: A Military Leader* (Phoenix Mill, England: Sutton Publishing Limited, 1999), p. 39.

6. Scott, p. 67.

7. Ibid., p. 125.

8. Sackville-West, p. 57.

9. Virginia Frohlick—Saint Joan of Arc Center, "Valcouleurs and Journey to Chinon," *Saint Joan of Arc's Trial of Nullification,* n.d., <http://www.stjoan-center.com/Trials/null04.html> (May 30, 2002).

10. Polly Schoyer Brooks, *Beyond the Myth: The Story of Joan of Arc* (New York: J. B. Lippincott, 1990), p. 37.

Chapter 4. Chinon

1. Vita Sackville-West, *Saint Joan of Arc* (London: The Folio Society, 1995), p. 99.

2. Lucien Fabre, *Joan of Arc,* trans. Gerard Hopkins (New York: McGraw-Hill Book Company, Inc., 1954), p. 113.

3. Régine Pernoud and Marie Véronique Clin, *Joan of Arc: Her Story* (New York: St. Martin's Press, 1998), p. 23.

4. Sackville-West, p. 109.

5. Pernoud and Clin, p. 28.

6. Virginia Frohlick—Saint Joan of Arc Center, "Arrival at Chinon and the Trial at Poitiers," *Saint Joan of*

Arc's Trial of Nullification, n.d., <http://www.stjoan-center.com/Trials/null05.html> (May 30, 2002).

7. Ibid.

8. Ibid.

9. Sackville-West, p. 116.

10. Virginia Frohlick—Saint Joan of Arc Center.

11. Sackville-West, p. 121.

Chapter 5. Orléans

1. Vita Sackville-West, *Saint Joan of Arc* (London: The Folio Society, 1995), p. 125.

2. Lucien Fabre, *Joan of Arc,* trans. Gerard Hopkins (New York: McGraw-Hill Book Company, Inc., 1954), p. 138.

3. Sackville-West, p. 133.

4. Ibid., p. 141.

5. Kelly DeVries, *Joan of Arc: A Military Leader* (Phoenix Mill, England: Sutton Publishing Limited, 1999), p. 79.

6. Fabre, p. 150.

7. Sackville-West, p. 151.

8. Régine Pernoud and Marie Véronique Clin, *Joan of Arc: Her Story* (New York: St. Martin's Press, 1998), p. 44.

9. Fabre, pp. 152–153.

10. Jay Williams, *Joan of Arc* (New York: American Heritage Publishing Company, 1963), p. 55.

11. Sackville-West, p. 154.

12. Fabre, p. 159.

13. Ibid., p. 164.

14. Virginia Frohlick—Saint Joan of Arc Center, "Orléans," *Saint Joan of Arc's Trial of Nullification,* n.d.,

<http://www.stjoan-center.com/Trials/null06.html> (May 30, 2002).

Chapter 6. Reims

1. Lucien Fabre, *Joan of Arc,* trans. Gerard Hopkins (New York: McGraw-Hill Book Company, Inc., 1954), p. 168.

2. Régine Pernoud and Marie Véronique Clin, *Joan of Arc: Her Story* (New York: St. Martin's Press, 1998), p. 53.

3. Virginia Frohlick—Saint Joan of Arc Center, "Orléans," *Saint Joan of Arc's Trial of Nullification,* n.d., <http://www.stjoan-center.com/Trials/null06.html> (May 30, 2002).

4. Virginia Frohlick—Saint Joan of Arc Center, "Joan's Friends Part 1," *Saint Joan of Arc's Trial of Nullification,* n.d., <http://www.stjoan-center.com/Trials/null07.html> (May 30, 2002).

5. Vita Sackville-West, *Saint Joan of Arc* (London: The Folio Society, 1995), p. 169.

6. Virginia Frohlick—Saint Joan of Arc Center, "Joan's Friends Part 1," *Saint Joan of Arc's Trial of Nullification,* n.d., <http://www.stjoan-center.com/Trials/null07.html> (May 30, 2002).

7. Fabre, p. 175.

8. Kelly DeVries, *Joan of Arc: A Military Leader* (Phoenix Mill, England: Sutton Publishing Limited, 1999), p. 112.

9. Virginia Frohlick—Saint Joan of Arc Center, "Orléans."

10. Ibid.

11. Pernoud and Clin, p. 66.

12. Fabre, p. 199.

Chapter 7. Paris and Compiègne

1. Virginia Frohlick—Saint Joan of Arc Center, "Arrival at Chinon and the Trial at Poitiers," *Saint Joan of Arc's Trial of Nullification,* n.d., <http://www.stjoan-center.com/Trials/null05.html> (May 30, 2002).

2. Régine Pernoud and Marie Véronique Clin, *Joan of Arc: Her Story* (New York: St. Martin's Press, 1998), p. 79.

3. Jay Williams, *Joan of Arc* (New York: American Heritage Publishing Company, 1963), p. 91.

4. Kelly DeVries, *Joan of Arc: A Military Leader* (Phoenix Mill, England: Sutton Publishing Limited, 1999), p. 144.

5. Régine Pernoud and Marie Véronique Clin, *Joan of Arc: Her Story* (New York: St. Martin's Press, 1998), p. 77.

6. Virginia Frohlick—Saint Joan of Arc Center, "The Private Examinations Begin," *Saint Joan of Arc's Trial of Condemnation,* n.d., <http://www.stjoan-center.com/Trials/sec07.html> (May 30, 2002).

7. Williams, p. 112.

Chapter 8. Rouen

1. Vita Sackville-West, *Saint Joan of Arc* (London: The Folio Society, 1995), p. 217.

2. Jay Williams, *Joan of Arc* (New York: American Heritage Publishing Company, 1963), p. 115.

3. Sackville-West, p. 219.

4. Régine Pernoud and Marie Véronique Clin, *Joan of Arc: Her Story* (New York: St. Martin's Press, 1998), p. 91.

5. Ibid., p. 107.

6. Virginia Frohlick—Saint Joan of Arc Center, "The Private Examinations Begin," *Saint Joan of Arc's Trial of Condemnation,* n.d., <http://www.stjoan-center.com/Trials/sec07.html> (May 30, 2002).

7. Ibid.

8. Virginia Frohlick—Saint Joan of Arc Center, "Fourth Public Examination," *Saint Joan of Arc's Trial of Condemnation,* n.d., <http://www.stjoan-center.com/Trials/sec04.html> (May 30, 2002).

9. Virginia Frohlick—Saint Joan of Arc Center, "Third Public Examination," *Saint Joan of Arc's Trial of Condemnation,* n.d., <http://www.stjoan-center.com/Trials/sec03.html> (May 30, 2002).

10. Virginia Frohlick—Saint Joan of Arc Center, "Rouen Testimony Part 3," *Saint Joan of Arc's Trial of Nullification,* n.d., <http://www.stjoan-center.com/Trials/null11.html> (May 30, 2002).

11. Virginia Frohlick—Saint Joan of Arc Center, "Seventh Private Examination," *Saint Joan of Arc's Trial of Condemnation,* n.d., <http://www.stjoan-center.com/Trials/sec11.html> (June 18, 2002).

12. Virginia Frohlick—Saint Joan of Arc Center, "Deliberations Held on May 9th, 12th, 19th and the Final Session and Sentence and Recantation," *Saint Joan of Arc's Trial of Condemnation,* n.d., <http://www.stjoan-center.com/Trials/sec20.html> (May 30, 2002).

13. Virginia Frohlick—Saint Joan of Arc Center, "Trial of Nullification, Continuation of the First Inquiry: 1449," *Saint Joan of Arc's Trial of Nullification,* n.d., <http://www.stjoan-center.com/Trials/null02.html> (May 30, 2002).

14. Virginia Frohlick—Saint Joan of Arc Center, "Rouen Testimony Part 1," *Saint Joan of Arc's Trial of Nullification,* n.d., <http://www.stjoan-center.com/Trials/null09.html> (May 30, 2002).

15. Virginia Frohlick—Saint Joan of Arc Center, "Rouen Testimony Part 3."

16. Virginia Frohlick—Saint Joan of Arc Center, "Second Process: The Relapse, the Final Adjudication and the Sentence of Death," *Saint Joan of Arc's Trial of Condemnation,* n.d., <http://www.stjoan-center.com/Trials/sec21.html> (May 30, 2002).

17. Virginia Frohlick—Saint Joan of Arc Center, "Trial of Nullification, Continuation of the First Inquiry: 1449."

18. Virginia Frohlick—Saint Joan of Arc Center, "Rouen Testimony Part 2," *Saint Joan of Arc's Trial of Nullification,* n.d., <http://www.stjoan-center.com/Trials/null10.html> (May 30, 2002).

19. Virginia Frohlick—Saint Joan of Arc Center, "Trial of Nullification, Continuation of the First Inquiry: 1449."

20. Ibid.

Chapter 9. The Triumph of France

1. Janet Shirley, trans., *A Parisian Journal (Journal d'un Bourgeois de Paris)* (Clarendon, England: Oxford Press, 1968), p. 307.

2. A.R. Meyers, ed., *English Historical Documents: 1327–1485* (New York: Oxford University Press, 1969), p. 271.

Chapter 10. Redemption and Legacy

1. Régine Pernoud and Marie Véronique Clin, *Joan of Arc: Her Story* (New York: St. Martin's Press, 1998), pp. 156–157.

2. Virginia Frohlick—Saint Joan of Arc Center, "Concluding Document," *Saint Joan of Arc's Trial of Nullification,* n.d., <http://www.stjoan-center.com/Trials/null13.html> (May 30, 2002).

Further Reading and Internet Addresses

Books

Brooks, Polly Schoyer. *Beyond the Myth: The Story of Joan of Arc.* New York: Houghton Mifflin Company, 1999.

Hodges, Margaret. *Joan of Arc: The Lily Maid.* New York: Holiday House, Inc., 1999.

Nardo, Don. *France.* Danbury, Conn.: Children's Press, 2000.

Roberts, Jeremy. *Joan of Arc.* Minneapolis, Minn.: The Lerner Publishing Group, 2000.

Wallace, Susan Helen. *Saint Joan of Arc: God's Soldier.* Boston: Pauline Books & Media, 2000.

Internet Addresses

Frohlick, Virginia. *Saint Joan of Arc Center.* n.d. <http://www.stjoan-center.com/>.

Halsall, Paul. "France: The Hundred Years War." *Internet Medieval Sourcebook.* © 1996. <http://www.fordham.edu/halsall/sbook1m.html>.

"Hundred Years War: Overview." *eHistory.com.* n.d. <http://www.ehistory.com/middleages/hundredyearswar/overview.cfm>.

Index

A

Agincourt, 21, 99, 103
Alençon, duke of, 42, 46, 49, 53, 65, 66, 68, 76–77, 78, 79, 80, 109
Arc, Joan of
  banner, 47, 58, 65, 70, 78–79, 82, 90
  birth and family, 27–28, 109
  capture of, 83
  at Chinon, 38–39
  execution of, 5–6, 8–9, 11, 98
  hearing voices, 8, 29, 30, 31, 33, 39, 43, 44, 46, 54, 56, 57, 65, 67, 70, 73, 77, 81, 88, 92, 93, 95, 96, 113
  legacy, 112–113
  Nullification Trial, 62, 66, 97, 109
  at Paris, 76–79
  questioned at Poitiers, 43–44, 46
  at Reims, 70–73, 74
  at Rouen, 30, 89–90
  as saint, 7–8, 11, 111
  Condemnation Trial, 5–6, 7–8, 11, 29, 30, 32, 71, 77, 87, 88–90, 92, 93–96, 97, 98
  at Valcouleurs, 33

B

Baudricourt, Robert de, 31, 33, 34, 36–37, 44

Bedford, duke of, 24, 46, 75–76, 87, 88–89, 99–100, 112
Black Death, 17
Bordeaux, 104, 105, 106, 107
Bureau, Jean, 102, 103, 104, 105

C

Castillon, Battle of, 105–107
Cauchon, Pierre (bishop of Beauvais), 8, 71, 87, 88–89, 92, 93–96, 98, 109
Charles VII, king of France, 21–26, 28, 31, 33, 34, 36, 38–44, 46, 52, 62, 63, 64, 65, 67–72, 74–77, 79–82, 86, 89, 99–105, 107, 108, 111, 112
Charles VI, king of France, 19, 20, 23, 24, 101
Compiègne, 76, 81, 82, 83, 85
Condemnation Trial, 5–6, 7–8, 11, 29, 30, 32, 71, 77, 87, 88–90, 92, 93–96, 97, 98
Crécy, Battle of, 16–17, 18, 21, 103

D

dauphin. See Charles VII, king of France.
Domrémy, 26–27, 28, 30, 33, 34, 73, 89, 109

E
Edward, the Black Prince,
  17, 19
Edward III, king of England,
  13–19, 21

F
Fastolf, John, 54, 67, 68, 69
Fierbois, 39, 47
Flavy, Guillaume de, 81,
  82–83
Fromingy, Battle of, 103

G
Gladsdale, William, 53–54, 61
Guyenne, 18, 24, 104, 105, 106

H
Henry V, king of England, 21,
  23, 102
Henry VI, king of England,
  24, 61, 87, 99, 101, 99

J
John, count of Dunois, 51–54,
  56, 57, 58, 61, 62
John the Fearless, 20, 22, 23
John II, king of France, 17–18

L
La Trémoïlle, Georges de,
  42–43, 64, 65, 68, 72, 75,
  76, 79, 80, 83, 86, 100, 109

M
Massieu, Jean, 8, 9, 92, 94, 95
Metz, Jean de, 34, 37, 38, 90

N
Nullification Trial, 62, 66, 97,
  109

O
Orléans, 20, 24–25, 31, 44, 46,
  47, 49, 50–55, 61, 62, 64,
  65, 67, 82, 109, 111, 112

P
Patay, Battle of, 69, 112
Philip of Burgundy, 20, 24–25,
  50, 69, 75, 80, 100
Philip of Valois, king of
  France, 13–14, 16, 17
Poitiers, Battle of, 17, 21, 44,
  46, 103
Poulengy, Bertrand de, 33, 34,
  37, 38, 43

R
Regnault of Chartres, 43, 64,
  65, 71, 72, 80, 83, 82, 86,
  109
Richemont, Arthur de, 67, 68,
  70, 101

S
Sluys, Battle of, 14

T
Talbot, John, 46, 50, 52, 54,
  61, 67–68, 69, 102, 103,
  104, 105
Treaty of Troyes, 23–24
Troyes, 70–71, 113

V
Vienne, Colet de, 36, 37, 38

W
Wandomme, Lionel of, 84, 87,
  88